PEARSON

COMMON CORE

Literature

Close Reading Notebook

GRADE 10

PEARSON

UPPER SADDLE RIVER, NEW JERSEY • BOSTON, MASSACHUSETTS
CHANDLER, ARIZONA • GLENVIEW, ILLINOIS

Acknowledgments appear on page 189, which constitutes an extension of this copyright page.

ISBN-13:   978-0-13-327569-8
ISBN-10:   0-13-327569-8
2 3 4 5 6 7 8 9 10 V039   17 16 15 14 13

CONTENTS

The Leap

by Louise Erdrich

TAKE NOTES

My mother is the surviving half of a blindfold trapeze act, not a fact I think about much even now that she is sightless, the result of encroaching and stubborn cataracts.

She walks slowly through her house here in New Hampshire, lightly touching her way along walls and running her hands over knickknacks, books, the drift of a grown child's belongings and castoffs. She has never upset an object or as much as brushed a magazine onto the floor. She has never lost her balance or bumped into a closet door left carelessly open.

It has occurred to me that the catlike precision of her movements in old age might be the result of her early training, but she shows so little of the drama or flair one might expect from a performer that I tend to forget the Flying Avalons. She has kept no sequined costume, no photographs, no fliers or posters from that part of her youth. I would, in fact, tend to think that all memory of double somersaults and heart-stopping catches had left her arms and legs were it not for the fact that sometimes, as I sit sewing in the room of the rebuilt house in which I slept as a child, I hear the crackle, catch a whiff of smoke from the stove downstairs, and suddenly the room goes dark, the stitches burn beneath my fingers, and I am sewing with a needle of hot silver, a thread of fire.

I owe her my existence three times. The first was when she saved herself. In the town square a replica tent pole, cracked and splintered, now stands cast in concrete. It commemorates the disaster that put our town smack on the front page of the Boston and New York tabloids. It is from those old newspapers, now historical records, that I get my information. Not from my mother, Anna of the Flying Avalons, nor from any of her in-laws, nor certainly from the other half of her particular act, Harold Avalon, her first husband. In one news account it says, "The day was mildly

TAKE NOTES

overcast, but nothing in the air or temperature gave any hint of the sudden force with which the deadly gale would strike."

I have lived in the West, where you can see the weather coming for miles, and it is true that out here we are at something of a disadvantage. When extremes of temperature collide, a hot and cold front, winds generate instantaneously behind a hill and crash upon you without warning. That, I think, was the likely situation on that day in June. People probably commented on the pleasant air, grateful that no hot sun beat upon the striped tent that stretched over the entire center green. They bought their tickets and surrendered them in anticipation. They sat. They ate caramelized popcorn and roasted peanuts. There was time, before the storm, for three acts. The White Arabians[1] of Ali-Khazar rose on their hind legs and waltzed. The Mysterious Bernie folded himself into a painted cracker tin, and the Lady of the Mists made herself appear and disappear in surprising places. As the clouds gathered outside, unnoticed, the ringmaster cracked his whip, shouted his introduction, and pointed to the ceiling of the tent, where the Flying Avalons were perched.

They loved to drop gracefully from nowhere, like two sparkling birds, and blow kisses as they threw off their plumed helmets and high-collared capes. They laughed and flirted openly as they beat their way up again on the trapeze bars. In the final vignette of their act, they actually would kiss in midair, pausing, almost hovering as they swooped past one another. On the ground, between bows, Harry Avalon would skip quickly to the front rows and point out the smear of my mother's lipstick, just off the edge of his mouth. They made a romantic pair all right, especially in the blindfold sequence.

That afternoon, as the anticipation increased, as Mr. and Mrs. Avalon tied sparkling strips of cloth onto each other's face and as they puckered their lips in mock kisses, lips destined "never again to meet," as one long breathless article put it, the wind rose, miles off, wrapped itself into a cone, and howled. There

---

1. **Arabians** horses of the Arabian breed.

came a rumble of electrical energy, drowned out by
the sudden roll of drums. One detail not mentioned
by the press, perhaps unknown—Anna was pregnant
at the time, seven months and hardly showing, her
stomach muscles were that strong. It seems incredible
that she would work high above the ground when any
fall could be so dangerous, but the explanation—I
know from watching her go blind—is that my mother
lives comfortably in extreme elements. She is one with
the constant dark now, just as the air was her home,
familiar to her, safe, before the storm that afternoon.

From opposite ends of the tent they waved, blind and
smiling, to the crowd below. The ringmaster removed
his hat and called for silence, so that the two above
could concentrate. They rubbed their hands in chalky
powder, then Harry launched himself and swung, once,
twice, in huge calibrated beats across space. He hung
from his knees and on the third swing stretched wide
his arms, held his hands out to receive his pregnant
wife as she dove from her shining bar.

It was while the two were in midair, their hands
about to meet, that lightning struck the main pole and
sizzled down the guy wires, filling the air with a blue
radiance that Harry Avalon must certainly have seen
through the cloth of his blindfold as the tent buckled
and the edifice[2] toppled him forward, the swing
continuing and not returning in its sweep, and Harry
going down, down into the crowd with his last thought,
perhaps, just a prickle of surprise at his empty hands.

My mother once said that I'd be amazed at how
many things a person can do within the act of falling.
Perhaps, at the time, she was teaching me to dive off
a board at the town pool, for I associate the idea with
midair somersaults. But I also think she meant that
even in that awful doomed second one could think,
for she certainly did. When her hands did not meet
her husband's, my mother tore her blindfold away.
As he swept past her on the wrong side, she could
have grasped his ankle, the toe-end of his tights,
and gone down clutching him. Instead, she changed
direction. Her body twisted toward a heavy wire and
she managed to hang on to the braided metal, still hot

---

2. edifice (ed´ i fis) *n.* large structure or building.

TAKE NOTES

from the lightning strike. Her palms were burned so terribly that once healed they bore no lines, only the blank scar tissue of a quieter future. She was lowered, gently, to the sawdust ring just underneath the dome of the canvas roof, which did not entirely settle but was held up on one end and jabbed through, torn, and still on fire in places from the giant spark, though rain and men's jackets soon put that out.

Three people died, but except for her hands my mother was not seriously harmed until an overeager rescuer broke her arm in extricating her and also, in the process, collapsed a portion of the tent bearing a huge buckle that knocked her unconscious. She was taken to the town hospital, and there she must have hemorrhaged,[3] for they kept her, confined to her bed, a month and a half before her baby was born without life.

Harry Avalon had wanted to be buried in the circus cemetery next to the original Avalon, his uncle, so she sent him back with his brothers. The child, however, is buried around the corner, beyond this house and just down the highway. Sometimes I used to walk there just to sit. She was a girl, but I rarely thought of her as a sister or even as a separate person really. I suppose you could call it the egocentrism[4] of a child, of all young children, but I considered her a less finished version of myself.

When the snow falls, throwing shadows among the stones, I can easily pick hers out from the road, for it is bigger than the others and in the shape of a lamb at rest, its legs curled beneath. The carved lamb looms larger as the years pass, though it is probably only my eyes, the vision shifting, as what is close to me blurs and distances sharpen. In odd moments, I think it is the edge drawing near, the edge of everything, the unseen horizon we do not really speak of in the eastern woods. And it also seems to me, although this is probably an idle fantasy, that the statue is growing more sharply etched, as if, instead of weathering itself into a porous mass, it is hardening on the hillside with each snowfall, perfecting itself.

---

3. **hemorrhaged** (hem′ ər ijd′) *v.* bled heavily.
4. **egocentrism** (ē′ gō sen′ triz əm) *n.* self-centeredness; inability to distinguish one's own needs and interests from those of others.

It was during her confinement in the hospital that my mother met my father. He was called in to look at the set of her arm, which was complicated. He stayed, sitting at her bedside, for he was something of an armchair traveler and had spent his war quietly, at an air force training grounds, where he became a specialist in arms and legs broken during parachute training exercises. Anna Avalon had been to many of the places he longed to visit—Venice, Rome, Mexico, all through France and Spain. She had no family of her own and was taken in by the Avalons, trained to perform from a very young age. They toured Europe before the war, then based themselves in New York. She was illiterate.

It was in the hospital that she finally learned to read and write, as a way of overcoming the boredom and depression of those weeks, and it was my father who insisted on teaching her. In return for stories of her adventures, he graded her first exercises. He bought her her first book, and over her bold letters, which the pale guides of the penmanship pads could not contain, they fell in love.

I wonder if my father calculated the exchange he offered: one form of flight for another. For after that, and for as long as I can remember, my mother has never been without a book. Until now, that is, and it remains the greatest difficulty of her blindness. Since my father's recent death, there is no one to read to her, which is why I returned, in fact, from my failed life where the land is flat. I came home to read to my mother, to read out loud, to read long into the dark if I must, to read all night.

Once my father and mother married, they moved onto the old farm he had inherited but didn't care much for. Though he'd been thinking of moving to a larger city, he settled down and broadened his practice in this valley. It still seems odd to me, when they could have gone anywhere else, that they chose to stay in the town where the disaster had occurred, and which my father in the first place had found so constricting. It was my mother who insisted upon it, after her child did not survive. And then, too, she loved the sagging farmhouse with its scrap of what was left of a vast acreage of woods and hidden hay fields that stretched to the game park.

TAKE NOTES

I owe my existence, the second time then, to the two of them and the hospital that brought them together. That is the debt we take for granted since none of us asks for life. It is only once we have it that we hang on so dearly.

I was seven the year the house caught fire, probably from standing ash. It can rekindle, and my father, forgetful around the house and perpetually exhausted from night hours on call, often emptied what he thought were ashes from cold stoves into wooden or cardboard containers. The fire could have started from a flaming box, or perhaps a buildup of creosote inside the chimney was the culprit. It started right around the stove, and the heart of the house was gutted. The baby-sitter, fallen asleep in my father's den on the first floor, woke to find the stairway to my upstairs room cut off by flames. She used the phone, then ran outside to stand beneath my window.

When my parents arrived, the town volunteers had drawn water from the fire pond and were spraying the outside of the house, preparing to go inside after me, not knowing at the time that there was only one staircase and that it was lost. On the other side of the house, the superannuated[5] extension ladder broke in half. Perhaps the clatter of it falling against the walls woke me, for I'd been asleep up to that point.

As soon as I awakened, in the small room that I now use for sewing, I smelled the smoke. I followed things by the letter then, was good at memorizing instructions, and so I did exactly what was taught in the second-grade home fire drill. I got up, I touched the back of my door before opening it. Finding it hot, I left it closed and stuffed my rolled-up rug beneath the crack. I did not hide under my bed or crawl into my closet. I put on my flannel robe, and then I sat down to wait.

Outside, my mother stood below my dark window and saw clearly that there was no rescue. Flames had pierced one side wall, and the glare of the fire lighted the massive limbs and trunk of the vigorous old elm that had probably been planted the year the house was built, a hundred years ago at least. No leaf touched the

---

5. **superannuated** (so͞o′ pər an′ yo͞o āt′ ed) *adj.* too old to be usable.

wall, and just one thin branch scraped the roof. From below, it looked as though even a squirrel would have had trouble jumping from the tree onto the house, for the breadth of that small branch was no bigger than my mother's wrist.

Standing there, beside Father, who was preparing to rush back around to the front of the house, my mother asked him to unzip her dress. When he wouldn't be bothered, she made him understand. He couldn't make his hands work, so she finally tore it off and stood there in her pearls and stockings. She directed one of the men to lean the broken half of the extension ladder up against the trunk of the tree. In surprise, he complied. She ascended. She vanished. Then she could be seen among the leafless branches of late November as she made her way up and, along her stomach, inched the length of a bough that curved above the branch that brushed the roof.

Once there, swaying, she stood and balanced. There were plenty of people in the crowd and many who still remember, or think they do, my mother's leap through the ice-dark air toward that thinnest extension, and how she broke the branch falling so that it cracked in her hands, cracked louder than the flames as she vaulted with it toward the edge of the roof, and how it hurtled down end over end without her, and their eyes went up, again, to see where she had flown.

I didn't see her leap through air, only heard the sudden thump and looked out my window. She was hanging by the backs of her heels from the new gutter we had put in that year, and she was smiling. I was not surprised to see her, she was so matter-of-fact. She tapped on the window. I remember how she did it, too. It was the friendliest tap, a bit tentative, as if she was afraid she had arrived too early at a friend's house. Then she gestured at the latch, and when I opened the window she told me to raise it wider and prop it up with the stick so it wouldn't crush her fingers. She swung down, caught the ledge, and crawled through the opening. Once she was in my room, I realized she had on only underclothing, a bra of the heavy stitched cotton women used to wear and step-in, lace-trimmed drawers. I remember feeling light-headed, of course, terribly relieved, and then embarrassed for her to be seen by the crowd undressed.

TAKE NOTES

I was still embarrassed as we flew out the window, toward earth, me in her lap, her toes pointed as we skimmed toward the painted target of the fire fighter's net.

I know that she's right. I knew it even then. As you fall there is time to think. Curled as I was, against her stomach, I was not startled by the cries of the crowd or the looming faces. The wind roared and beat its hot breath at our back, the flames whistled. I slowly wondered what would happen if we missed the circle or bounced out of it. Then I wrapped my hands around my mother's hands. I felt the brush of her lips and heard the beat of her heart in my ears, loud as thunder, long as the roll of drums.

The Monkey's Paw

by W. W. Jacobs

I

Without, the night was cold and wet, but in the small parlor of Laburnam Villa the blinds were drawn and the fire burned brightly. Father and son were at chess, the former, who possessed ideas about the game involving radical changes, putting his king into such sharp and unnecessary perils that it even provoked comment from the white-haired old lady knitting placidly by the fire.

"Hark at the wind," said Mr. White, who, having seen a fatal mistake after it was too late, was amiably desirous of preventing his son from seeing it.

"I'm listening," said the latter, grimly surveying the board as he stretched out his hand. "Check."

"I should hardly think that he'd come tonight," said his father, with his hand poised over the board.

"Mate,"[1] replied the son.

"That's the worst of living so far out," bawled Mr. White, with sudden and unlooked-for violence; "of all the beastly, slushy, out-of-the-way places to live in, this is the worst. Pathway's a bog, and the road's a torrent. I don't know what people are thinking about. I suppose because only two houses on the road are let, they think it doesn't matter."

"Never mind, dear," said his wife, soothingly; "perhaps you'll win the next one."

Mr. White looked up sharply, just in time to intercept a knowing glance between mother and son. The words died away on his lips, and he hid a guilty grin in his thin gray beard.

"There he is," said Herbert White, as the gate banged to loudly and heavy footsteps came toward the door.

---

1. mate *n.* checkmate, a chess move that prevents the opponent's king from escaping capture and so ends the game.

TAKE NOTES

The old man rose with hospitable haste, and opening the door, was heard condoling with the new arrival. The new arrival also condoled with himself, so that Mrs. White said, "Tut, tut!" and coughed gently as her husband entered the room, followed by a tall, burly man, beady of eye and rubicund of visage.[2]

"Sergeant Major Morris," he said, introducing him.

The sergeant major shook hands, and taking the proffered seat by the fire, watched contentedly while his host got out tumblers and stood a small copper kettle on the fire.

At the third glass his eyes got brighter, and he began to talk, the little family circle regarding with eager interest this visitor from distant parts, as he squared his broad shoulders in the chair and spoke of wild scenes and doughty[3] deeds; of wars and plagues and strange peoples.

"Twenty-one years of it," said Mr. White, nodding at his wife and son. "When he went away he was a slip of a youth in the warehouse. Now look at him."

"He don't look to have taken much harm," said Mrs. White, politely.

"I'd like to go to India myself," said the old man, "just to look round a bit, you know."

"Better where you are," said the sergeant major, shaking his head. He put down the empty glass, and sighing softly, shook it again.

"I should like to see those old temples and fakirs and jugglers," said the old man. "What was that you started telling me the other day about a monkey's paw or something, Morris?"

"Nothing," said the soldier, hastily. "Leastways nothing worth hearing."

"Monkey's paw?" said Mrs. White, curiously.

"Well, it's just a bit of what you might call magic, perhaps," said the sergeant major, offhandedly.

His three listeners leaned forward eagerly. The visitor absent-mindedly put his empty glass to his lips and then set it down again. His host filled it for him.

"To look at," said the sergeant major, fumbling in his pocket, "it's just an ordinary little paw, dried to a mummy."

---

2. **rubicund** (rōō′ bə kund′) **of visage** (viz′ ij) having a red face.
3. **doughty** (dout′ ē) *adj.* brave.

He took something out of his pocket and proffered it. Mrs. White drew back with a grimace, but her son, taking it, examined it curiously.

"And what is there special about it?" inquired Mr. White as he took it from his son, and having examined it, placed it upon the table.

"It had a spell put on it by an old fakir," said the sergeant major, "a very holy man. He wanted to show that fate ruled people's lives, and that those who interfered with it did so to their sorrow. He put a spell on it so that three separate men could each have three wishes from it."

His manner was so impressive that his hearers were conscious that their light laughter jarred somewhat.

"Well, why don't you have three, sir?" said Herbert White, cleverly.

The soldier regarded him in the way that middle age is wont to regard presumptuous youth. "I have," he said, quietly, and his blotchy face whitened.

"And did you really have the three wishes granted?" asked Mrs. White.

"I did," said the sergeant major, and his glass tapped against his strong teeth.

"And has anybody else wished?" persisted the old lady.

"The first man had his three wishes, yes," was the reply; "I don't know what the first two were, but the third was for death. That's how I got the paw."

His tones were so grave that a hush fell upon the group.

"If you've had your three wishes, it's no good to you now, then, Morris," said the old man at last. "What do you keep it for?"

The soldier shook his head. "Fancy, I suppose," he said, slowly. "I did have some idea of selling it, but I don't think I will. It has caused enough mischief already. Besides, people won't buy. They think it's a fairy tale, some of them, and those who do think anything of it want to try it first and pay me afterward."

"If you could have another three wishes," said the old man, eyeing him keenly, "would you have them?"

"I don't know," said the other. "I don't know."

He took the paw, and dangling it between his forefinger and thumb, suddenly threw it upon the fire.

TAKE NOTES

White, with a slight cry, stooped down and snatched it off.

"Better let it burn," said the soldier, solemnly.

"If you don't want it, Morris," said the other, "give it to me."

"I won't," said his friend doggedly. "I threw it on the fire. If you keep it, don't blame me for what happens. Pitch it on the fire again, like a sensible man."

The other shook his head and examined his new possession closely. "How do you do it?" he inquired.

"Hold it up in your right hand and wish aloud," said the sergeant major, "but I warn you of the consequences."

"Sounds like the *Arabian Nights*,"[4] said Mrs. White, as she rose and began to set the supper. "Don't you think you might wish for four pairs of hands for me?"

Her husband drew the talisman from his pocket, and then all three burst into laughter as the sergeant major, with a look of alarm on his face, caught him by the arm. "If you must wish," he said, gruffly, "wish for something sensible."

Mr. White dropped it back in his pocket, and placing chairs, motioned his friend to the table. In the business of supper the talisman was partly forgotten, and afterward the three sat listening in an enthralled fashion to a second installment of the soldier's adventures in India.

"If the tale about the monkey's paw is not more truthful than those he has been telling us," said Herbert, as the door closed behind their guest, just in time for him to catch the last train, "we shan't make much out of it."

"Did you give him anything for it, Father?" inquired Mrs. White, regarding her husband closely.

"A trifle," said he, coloring slightly. "He didn't want it, but I made him take it. And he pressed me again to throw it away."

"Likely," said Herbert, with pretended horror. "Why, we're going to be rich, and famous and happy. Wish to be an emperor, Father, to begin with; then you can't be bossed around."

---

4. *Arabian Nights* collection of stories from the ancient Near East telling of fantastical adventures and supernatural beings.

He darted round the table, pursued by the maligned Mrs. White armed with an antimacassar.[5]

Mr. White took the paw from his pocket and eyed it dubiously. "I don't know what to wish for, and that's a fact," he said, slowly. "It seems to me I've got all I want."

"If you only cleared the house, you'd be quite happy, wouldn't you?" said Herbert, with his hand on his shoulder. "Well, wish for two hundred pounds,[6] then; that'll just do it."

His father, smiling shamefacedly at his own credulity, held up the talisman, as his son, with a solemn face somewhat marred by a wink at his mother, sat down at the piano and struck a few impressive chords.

"I wish for two hundred pounds," said the old man distinctly.

A fine crash from the piano greeted the words, interrupted by a shuddering cry from the old man. His wife and son ran toward him.

"It moved," he cried, with a glance of disgust at the object as it lay on the floor. "As I wished it twisted in my hand like a snake."

"Well, I don't see the money," said his son as he picked it up and placed it on the table, "and I bet I never shall."

"It must have been your fancy, Father," said his wife, regarding him anxiously.

He shook his head. "Never mind, though; there's no harm done, but it gave me a shock all the same."

They sat down by the fire again while the two men finished their pipes. Outside, the wind was higher than ever, and the old man started nervously at the sound of a door banging upstairs. A silence unusual and depressing settled upon all three, which lasted until the old couple rose to retire for the night.

"I expect you'll find the cash tied up in a big bag in the middle of your bed," said Herbert, as he bade them good night, "and something horrible squatting up on top of the wardrobe watching you as you pocket your ill-gotten gains."

---

5. **antimacassar** (anʹ ti mə kasʹ ər) *n.* small cover for the arms or back of a chair or sofa.
6. **pounds** *n.* units of English currency, roughly comparable to dollars.

Herbert sat alone in the darkness, gazing at the dying fire, and seeing faces in it. The last face was so horrible and so simian[7] that he gazed at it in amazement. It got so vivid that, with a little uneasy laugh, he felt on the table for a glass containing a little water to throw over it. His hand grasped the monkey's paw, and with a little shiver he wiped his hand on his coat and went up to bed. •

II

In the brightness of the wintry sun next morning as it streamed over the breakfast table Herbert laughed at his fears. There was an air of prosaic wholesomeness about the room which it had lacked on the previous night, and the dirty, shriveled little paw was pitched on the sideboard with a carelessness which betokened no great belief in its virtues.

"I suppose all old soldiers are the same," said Mrs. White. "The idea of our listening to such nonsense! How could wishes be granted in these days? And if they could, how could two hundred pounds hurt you, Father?"

"Might drop on his head from the sky," said the frivolous Herbert.

"Morris said the things happened so naturally," said his father, "that you might if you so wished attribute it to coincidence."

"Well, don't break into the money before I come back," said Herbert, as he rose from the table. "I'm afraid it'll turn you into a mean, avaricious[8] man, and we shall have to disown you."

His mother laughed, and following him to the door, watched him down the road, and, returning to the breakfast table, was very happy at the expense of her husband's credulity. All of which did not prevent her from scurrying to the door at the postman's knock, nor prevent her from referring somewhat shortly to retired sergeant majors of bibulous habits when she found that the post brought a tailor's bill.

"Herbert will have some more of his funny remarks, I expect, when he comes home," she said, as they sat at dinner.

---

7. **simian** (sim′ ē ən) *adj.* monkeylike.
8. **avaricious** (av′ ə rish′ əs) *adj.* greedy for wealth.

"I dare say," said Mr. White, "but for all that, the thing moved in my hand; that I'll swear to."

"You thought it did," said the old lady soothingly.

"I say it did," replied the other. "There was no thought about it; I had just—What's the matter?"

His wife made no reply. She was watching the mysterious movements of a man outside, who, peering in an undecided fashion at the house, appeared to be trying to make up his mind to enter. In mental connection with the two hundred pounds, she noticed that the stranger was well dressed, and wore a silk hat of glossy newness. Three times he paused at the gate, and then walked on again. The fourth time he stood with his hand upon it, and then with sudden resolution flung it open and walked up the path. Mrs. White at the same moment placed her hands behind her, and hurriedly unfastening the strings of her apron, put that useful article of apparel beneath the cushion of her chair.

She brought the stranger, who seemed ill at ease, into the room. He gazed at her furtively, and listened in a preoccupied fashion as the old lady apologized for the appearance of the room, and her husband's coat, a garment which he usually reserved for the garden. She then waited patiently for him to broach his business, but he was at first strangely silent.

"I—was asked to call," he said at last, and stooped and picked a piece of cotton from his trousers. "I come from 'Maw and Meggins.'"

The old lady started. "Is anything the matter?" she asked, breathlessly. "Has anything happened to Herbert? What is it? What is it?"

Her husband interposed. "There, there, mother," he said, hastily. "Sit down, and don't jump to conclusions. You've not brought bad news, I'm sure, sir," and he eyed the other wistfully.

"I'm sorry—" began the visitor.

"Is he hurt?" demanded the mother, wildly.

The visitor bowed in assent. "Badly hurt," he said quietly, "but he is not in any pain."

"Oh, thank God!" said the old woman, clasping her hands. "Thank God for that! Thank—"

She broke off suddenly as the sinister meaning of the assurance dawned upon her and she saw the awful

TAKE NOTES

confirmation of her fears in the other's averted face. She caught her breath, and turning to her husband, laid her trembling old hand upon his. There was a long silence.

"He was caught in the machinery," said the visitor at length, in a low voice.

"Caught in the machinery," repeated Mr. White, in a dazed fashion, "yes."

He sat staring blankly out at the window, and taking his wife's hand between his own, pressed it as he had been wont to do in their old courting days nearly forty years before.

"He was the only one left to us," he said, turning gently to the visitor. "It is hard."

The other coughed, and, rising, walked slowly to the window. "The firm wished me to convey their sincere sympathy with you in your great loss," he said, without looking round. "I beg that you will understand I am only their servant and merely obeying orders."

There was no reply; the old woman's face was white, her eyes staring, and her breath inaudible; on the husband's face was a look such as his friend the sergeant might have carried into his first action.

"I was to say that Maw and Meggins disclaim all responsibility," continued the other. "They admit no liability at all, but in consideration of your son's services they wish to present you with a certain sum as compensation."

Mr. White dropped his wife's hand, and rising to his feet, gazed with a look of horror at his visitor. His dry lips shaped the words, "How much?"

"Two hundred pounds," was the answer.

Unconscious of his wife's shriek, the old man smiled faintly, put out his hands like a sightless man, and dropped, a senseless heap, to the floor. •

III

In the huge new cemetery, some two miles distant, the old people buried their dead, and came back to a house steeped in shadow and silence. It was all over so quickly that at first they could hardly realize it, and remained in a state of expectation as though of something else to happen—something else which was to lighten this load, too heavy for old hearts to bear.

But the days passed, and expectation gave place to resignation—the hopeless resignation of the old, sometimes miscalled apathy. Sometimes they hardly exchanged a word, for now they had nothing to talk about, and their days were long to weariness.

It was about a week after that the old man, waking suddenly in the night, stretched out his hand and found himself alone. The room was in darkness, and the sound of subdued weeping came from the window. He raised himself in bed and listened.

"Come back," he said, tenderly. "You will be cold."

"It is colder for my son," said the old woman, and wept afresh.

The sound of her sobs died away on his ears. The bed was warm, and his eyes heavy with sleep. He dozed fitfully, and then slept until a sudden wild cry from his wife awoke him with a start.

"*The paw!*" she cried wildly. "The monkey's paw!"

He started up in alarm. "Where? Where is it? What's the matter?"

She came stumbling across the room toward him. "I want it," she said quietly. "You've not destroyed it?"

"It's in the parlor, on the bracket," he replied, marveling. "Why?"

She cried and laughed together, and bending over, kissed his cheek.

"I only just thought of it," she said hysterically. "Why didn't I think of it before? Why didn't *you* think of it?"

"Think of what?" he questioned.

"The other two wishes," she replied rapidly. "We've only had one."

"Was not that enough?" he demanded, fiercely.

"No," she cried triumphantly; "we'll have one more. Go down and get it quickly, and wish our boy alive again."

The man sat up in bed and flung the bedclothes from his quaking limbs. "You are mad!" he cried, aghast.

"Get it," she panted; "get it quickly, and wish—Oh, my boy, my boy!"

Her husband struck a match and lit the candle. "Get back to bed," he said unsteadily. "You don't know what you are saying."

"We had the first wish granted," said the old woman feverishly; "why not the second?"

TAKE NOTES

TAKE NOTES

____
____
____
____
____
____
____
____
____
____
____
____
____
____
____
____
____
____
____
____
____
____
____
____

"A coincidence," stammered the old man.

"Go and get it and wish," cried his wife, quivering with excitement.

The old man turned and regarded her, and his voice shook. "He has been dead ten days, and besides he—I would not tell you else, but—I could only recognize him by his clothing. If he was too terrible for you to see then, how now?"

"Bring him back," cried the old woman, and dragged him toward the door. "Do you think I fear the child I have nursed?"

He went down in the darkness, and felt his way to the parlor, and then to the mantelpiece. The talisman was in its place, and a horrible fear that the unspoken wish might bring his mutilated son before him ere he could escape from the room seized upon him, and he caught his breath as he found that he had lost the direction of the door. His brow cold with sweat, he felt his way round the table, and groped along the wall until he found himself in the small passage with the unwholesome thing in his hand.

Even his wife's face seemed changed as he entered the room. It was white and expectant, and to his fears seemed to have an unnatural look upon it. He was afraid of her.

"_Wish!_" she cried, in a strong voice.

"It is foolish and wicked," he faltered.

"_Wish!_" repeated his wife.

He raised his hand. "I wish my son alive again."

The talisman fell to the floor, and he regarded it fearfully. Then he sank trembling into a chair as the old woman, with burning eyes, walked to the window and raised the blind.

He sat until he was chilled with the cold, glancing occasionally at the figure of the old woman peering through the window. The candle-end, which had burned below the rim of the china candlestick, was throwing pulsating shadows on the ceiling and walls, until, with a flicker larger than the rest, it expired. The old man, with an unspeakable sense of relief at the failure of the talisman, crept back to his bed, and a minute or two afterward the old woman came silently and apathetically beside him.

Neither spoke, but lay silently listening to the ticking of the clock. A stair creaked, and a squeaky mouse scurried noisily through the wall. The darkness was oppressive, and after lying for some time screwing up his courage, he took the box of matches, and striking one, went downstairs for a candle.

At the foot of the stairs the match went out, and he paused to strike another; and at the same moment a knock, so quiet and stealthy as to be scarcely audible, sounded on the front door.

The matches fell from his hand and spilled in the passage. He stood motionless, his breath suspended until the knock was repeated. Then he turned and fled swiftly back to his room, and closed the door behind him. A third knock sounded through the house.

"*What's that?*" cried the old woman, starting up.

"A rat," said the old man in shaking tones—"a rat. It passed me on the stairs."

His wife sat up in bed listening. A loud knock resounded through the house.

"It's Herbert!" she screamed. "It's Herbert!"

She ran to the door, but her husband was before her, and catching her by the arm, held her tightly.

"What are you going to do?" he whispered hoarsely.

"It's my boy; it's Herbert!" she cried, struggling mechanically. "I forgot it was two miles away. What are you holding me for? Let go. I must open the door."

"Don't let it in," cried the old man, trembling.

"You're afraid of your own son," she cried, struggling. "Let me go. I'm coming, Herbert, I'm coming."

There was another knock, and another. The old woman with a sudden wrench broke free and ran from the room. Her husband followed to the landing, and called after her appealingly as she hurried downstairs. He heard the chain rattle back and the bottom bolt drawn slowly and stiffly from the socket. Then the old woman's voice, strained and panting.

"The bolt," she cried, loudly. "Come down. I can't reach it."

But her husband was on his hands and knees groping wildly on the floor in search of the paw. If he could only find it before the thing outside got in. A perfect fusillade[9] of knocks reverberated through the house, and he heard the scraping of a chair as his wife

---

9. fusillade (fyo͞o′ sə lād′) *n.* rapid firing, as of gunshots.

TAKE NOTES

put it down in the passage against the door. He heard the creaking of the bolt as it came slowly back, and at the same moment he found the monkey's paw, and frantically breathed his third and last wish.

The knocking ceased suddenly, although the echoes of it were still in the house. He heard the chair drawn back and the door opened. A cold wind rushed up the staircase, and a long loud wail of disappointment and misery from his wife gave him courage to run down to her side, and then to the gate beyond. The street lamp flickering opposite shone on a quiet and deserted road.

The Street of the Cañon

by Josephina Niggli

TAKE NOTES

It was May, the flowering thorn was sweet in the air, and the village of San Juan Iglesias in the Valley of the Three Marys was celebrating. The long dark streets were empty because all of the people, from the lowest-paid cowboy to the mayor, were helping Don Roméo Calderón celebrate his daughter's eighteenth birthday.

On the other side of the town, where the Cañon Road led across the mountains to the Sabinas Valley, a tall slender man, a package clutched tightly against his side, slipped from shadow to shadow. Once a dog barked, and the man's black suit merged into the blackness of a wall. But no voice called out, and after a moment he slid into the narrow, dirt-packed street again.

The moonlight touched his shoulder and spilled across his narrow hips. He was young, no more than twenty-five, and his black curly head was bare. He walked swiftly along, heading always for the distant sound of guitar and flute. If he met anyone now, who could say from which direction he had come? He might be a trader from Monterrey, or a buyer of cow's milk from farther north in the Valley of the Three Marys. Who would guess that an Hidalgo man dared to walk alone in the moonlit streets of San Juan Iglesias?

Carefully adjusting his flat package so that it was not too prominent, he squared his shoulders and walked jauntily across the street to the laughter-filled house. Little boys packed in the doorway made way for him, smiling and nodding to him. The long, narrow room with the orchestra at one end was filled with whirling dancers. Rigid-backed chaperones[1] were gossiping together, seated in their straight chairs against the plaster

---

1. **chaperones** (shap´ ər ōnz´) older or married women who accompany and supervise the behavior of a young person in public.

TAKE NOTES

walls. Over the scene was the yellow glow of kerosene lanterns, and the air was hot with the too-sweet perfume of gardenias, tuberoses,[2] and the pungent scent of close-packed humanity.

The man in the doorway, while trying to appear at ease, was carefully examining every smiling face. If just one person recognized him, the room would turn on him like a den of snarling mountain cats, but so far all the laughter-dancing eyes were friendly.

Suddenly a plump, officious little man, his round cheeks glistening with perspiration, pushed his way through the crowd. His voice, many times too large for his small body, boomed at the man in the doorway. "Welcome, stranger, welcome to our house." Thrusting his arm through the stranger's, and almost dislodging the package, he started to lead the way through the maze of dancers. "Come and drink a toast to my daughter—to my beautiful Sarita. She is eighteen this night."

In the square patio the gentle breeze ruffled the pink and white oleander bushes. A long table set up on sawhorses held loaves of flaky crusted French bread, stacks of thin, delicate tortillas, plates of barbecued beef, and long red rolls of spicy sausages. But most of all there were cheeses, for the Three Marys was a cheese-eating valley. There were yellow cheese and white cheese and curded cheese from cow's milk. There was even a flat white cake of goat cheese from distant Linares, a delicacy too expensive for any but feast days.

To set off this feast were bottles of beer floating in ice-filled tin tubs, and another table was covered with bottles of mescal, of tequila, of maguey wine.

Don Roméo Calderón thrust a glass of tequila into the stranger's hand. "Drink, friend, to the prettiest girl in San Juan. As pretty as my fine fighting cocks, she is. On her wedding day she takes to her man, and may she find him soon, the best fighter in my flock. Drink deep, friend. Even the rivers flow with wine."

The Hidalgo man laughed and raised his glass high. "May the earth be always fertile beneath her feet."

---

2. **gardenias** (gär dēn´ yəz), **tuberoses** (tōob´ rōz´ əs) two types of plant with especially sweet-smelling flowers.

Someone called to Don Roméo that more guests were arriving, and with a final delighted pat on the stranger's shoulder, the little man scurried away. As the young fellow smiled after his retreating host, his eyes caught and held another pair of eyes—laughing black eyes set in a young girl's face. The last time he had seen that face it had been white and tense with rage, and the lips clenched tight to prevent an outgushing stream of angry words. That had been in February, and she had worn a white lace shawl over her hair. Now it was May, and a gardenia was a splash of white in the glossy dark braids. The moonlight had mottled his face that February night, and he knew that she did not recognize him. He grinned impudently[3] back at her, and her eyes widened, then slid sideways to one of the chaperones. The fan in her small hand snapped shut. She tapped its parchment tip against her mouth and slipped away to join the dancing couples in the front room. The gestures of a fan translate into a coded language on the frontier. The stranger raised one eyebrow as he interpreted the signal.

But he did not move toward her at once. Instead, he inched slowly back against the table. No one was behind him, and his hands quickly unfastened the package he had been guarding so long. Then he nonchalantly walked into the front room.

The girl was sitting close to a chaperone. As he came up to her he swerved slightly toward the bushy-browed old lady.

"Your servant, señora. I kiss your hands and feet."

The chaperone stared at him in astonishment. Such fine manners were not common to the town of San Juan Iglesias.

"Eh, you're a stranger," she said. "I thought so."

"But a stranger no longer, señora, now that I have met you." He bent over her, so close she could smell the faint fragrance of talcum on his freshly shaven cheek.

"Will you dance the *parada* with me?"

This request startled her eyes into popping open beneath the heavy brows. "So, my young rooster,

---

3. impudently (im′ pyōō dənt lē) *adv.* in a shamelessly bold or provocative way.

TAKE NOTES

would you flirt with me, and I old enough to be your grandmother?"

"Can you show me a prettier woman to flirt with in the Valley of the Three Marys?" he asked audaciously.

She grinned at him and turned toward the girl at her side. "This young fool wants to meet you, my child."

The girl blushed to the roots of her hair and shyly lowered her white lids. The old woman laughed aloud.

"Go out and dance, the two of you. A man clever enough to pat the sheep has a right to play with the lamb."

The next moment they had joined the circle of dancers and Sarita was trying to control her laughter.

"She is the worst dragon in San Juan. And how easily you won her!"

"What is a dragon," he asked imperiously, "when I longed to dance with you?"

"Ay," she retorted, "you have a quick tongue. I think you are a dangerous man."

In answer he drew her closer to him, and turned her toward the orchestra. As he reached the chief violinist he called out, "Play the Virgencita, 'The Shy Young Maiden.'"

The violinist's mouth opened in soundless surprise. The girl in his arms said sharply, "You heard him, the *Borachita*, 'The Little Drunken Girl.'"

With a relieved grin, the violinist tapped his music stand with his bow, and the music swung into the sad farewell of a man to his sweetheart:

> *Farewell, my little drunken one,*
> *I must go to the capital*
> *To serve the master*
> *Who makes me weep for my return.*

The stranger frowned down at her. "Is this a joke, señorita?" he asked coldly.

"No," she whispered, looking about her quickly to see if the incident had been observed. "But the Virgencita is the favorite song of Hidalgo, a village on the other side of the mountains in the next valley. The people of Hidalgo and San Juan Iglesias do not speak."

"That is a stupid thing," said the man from Hidalgo as he swung her around in a large turn. "Is not music

free as air? Why should one town own the rights to
a song?"

The girl shuddered slightly. "Those people from
Hidalgo—they are wicked monsters. Can you guess
what they did not six months since?"

The man started to point out that the space of
time from February to May was three months, but he
thought it better not to appear too wise. "Did these
Hidalgo monsters frighten you, señorita? If they did, I
personally will kill them all."

She moved closer against him and tilted her face
until her mouth was close to his ear. "They attempted
to steal the bones of Don Rómolo Balderas."

"Is it possible?" He made his eyes grow round and
his lips purse up in disdain. "Surely not that! Why, all
the world knows that Don Rómolo Balderas was the
greatest historian in the entire Republic. Every school
child reads his books. Wise men from Quintana Roo
to the Río Bravo bow their heads in admiration to
his name. What a wicked thing to do!" He hoped his
virtuous tone was not too virtuous for plausibility, but
she did not seem to notice.

"It is true! In the night they came. Three devils!"

"Young devils, I hope."

"Young or old, who cares? They were devils. The
blacksmith surprised them even as they were opening
the grave. He raised such a shout that all of San Juan
rushed to his aid, for they were fighting, I can tell you.
Especially one of them—their leader."

"And who was he?"

"You have heard of him doubtless. A proper wild one
named Pepe Gonzalez."

"And what happened to them?"

"They had horses and got away, but one, I think,
was hurt."

The Hidalgo man twisted his mouth remembering
how Rubén the candymaker had ridden across
the whitewashed line high on the cañon trail
that marked the division between the Three Marys'
and the Sabinas' sides of the mountains, and then
had fallen in a faint from his saddle because his left
arm was broken. There was no candy in Hidalgo for
six weeks, and the entire Sabinas Valley resented that
broken arm as fiercely as did Rubén.

TAKE NOTES

The stranger tightened his arm in reflexed anger about Sarita's waist as she said, "All the world knows that the men of Hidalgo are sons of the mountain witches."

"But even devils are shy of disturbing the honored dead," he said gravely.

"'Don Rómolo was born in our village,' Hidalgo says. 'His bones belong to us.' Well, anyone in the valley can tell you he died in San Juan Iglesias, and here his bones will stay! Is that not proper? Is that not right?"

To keep from answering, he guided her through an intricate dance pattern that led them past the patio door. Over her head he could see two men and a woman staring with amazement at the open package on the table.

His eyes on the patio, he asked blandly, "You say the leader was one Pepe Gonzalez? The name seems to have a familiar sound."

"But naturally. He has a talent." She tossed her head and stepped away from him as the music stopped. It was a dance of two *paradas.* He slipped his hand through her arm and guided her into place in the large oval of parading couples. Twice around the room and the orchestra would play again.

"A talent?" he prompted.

"For doing the impossible. When all the world says a thing cannot be done, he does it to prove the world wrong. Why, he climbed to the top of the Prow, and not even the long vanished Joaquín Castillo had ever climbed that mountain before. And this same Pepe caught a mountain lion with nothing to aid him but a rope and his two bare hands."

"He doesn't sound such a bad friend," protested the stranger, slipping his arm around her waist as the music began to play the merry song of the soap bubbles:

> *Pretty bubbles of a thousand colors*
> *That ride on the wind*
> *And break as swiftly*
> *As a lover's heart.*

The events in the patio were claiming his attention. Little by little he edged her closer to the door. The group at the table had considerably enlarged. There was a low murmur of excitement from the crowd.

"What has happened?" asked Sarita, attracted by the noise.

"There seems to be something wrong at the table," he answered, while trying to peer over the heads of the people in front of him. Realizing that this might be the last moment of peace he would have that evening, he bent toward her.

"If I come back on Sunday, will you walk around the plaza with me?"

She was startled into exclaiming, "Ay, no!"

"Please. Just once around."

"And you think I'd walk more than once with you, señor, even if you were no stranger? In San Juan Iglesias, to walk around the plaza with a girl means a wedding."

"Ha, and you think that is common to San Juan alone? Even the devils of Hidalgo respect that law," he added hastily at her puzzled upward glance. "And so they do in all the villages." To cover his lapse[4] he said softly, "I don't even know your name."

A mischievous grin crinkled the corners of her eyes. "Nor do I know yours, señor. Strangers do not often walk the streets of San Juan."

Before he could answer, the chattering in the patio swelled to louder proportions. Don Roméo's voice lay on top, like thick cream on milk. "I tell you it is a jewel of a cheese. Such flavor, such texture, such whiteness. It is a jewel of a cheese."

"What has happened?" Sarita asked of a woman at her elbow.

"A fine goat's cheese appeared as if by magic on the table. No one knows where it came from."

"Probably an extra one from Linares," snorted a fat bald man on the right.

"Linares never made such a cheese as this," said the woman decisively.

"Silence!" roared Don Roméo. "Old Tío Daniel would speak a word to us."

A great hand of silence closed down over the mouths of the people. The girl was standing on tiptoe trying

---

4. **lapse** (laps) *n.* slip; error.

TAKE NOTES

vainly to see what was happening. She was hardly aware of the stranger's whispering voice although she remembered the words that he said. "Sunday night—once around the plaza."

She did not realize that he had moved away, leaving a gap that was quickly filled by the blacksmith.

Old Tío Daniel's voice was a shrill squeak, and his thin, stringy neck jutted forth from his body like a turtle's from its shell. "This is no cheese from Linares," he said with authority, his mouth sucking in over his toothless gums between his sentences. "Years ago, when the great Don Rómolo Balderas was still alive, we had such cheese as this—ay, in those days we had it. But after he died and was buried in our own sainted ground, as was right and proper . . ."

"Yes, yes," muttered voices in the crowd. He glared at the interruption. As soon as there was silence again, he continued:

"After he died, we had it no more. Shall I tell you why?"

"Tell us, Tío Daniel," said the voices humbly.

"Because it is made in Hidalgo!"

The sound of a waterfall, the sound of a wind in a narrow cañon, and the sound of an angry crowd are much the same. There were no distinct words, but the sound was enough.

"Are you certain, Tío?" boomed Don Roméo.

"As certain as I am that a donkey has long ears. The people of Hidalgo have been famous for generations for making cheese like this—especially that wicked one, that owner of a cheese factory, Timotéo Gonzalez, father to Pepe, the wild one, whom we have good cause to remember."

"We do, we do," came the sigh of assurance.

"But on the whole northern frontier there are no vats like his to produce so fine a product. Ask the people of Chihuahua, of Sonora. Ask the man on the bridge at Laredo, or the man in his boat at Tampico, 'Hola, friend, who makes the finest goat cheese?' And the answer will always be the same, 'Don Timotéo of Hidalgo.'"

It was the blacksmith who asked the great question. "Then where did that cheese come from, and we haters of Hidalgo these ten long years?"

No voice said, "The stranger," but with one fluid movement every head in the patio turned toward the girl in the doorway. She also turned, her eyes wide with something that she realized to her own amazement was more apprehension than anger.

But the stranger was not in the room. When the angry, muttering men pushed through to the street, the stranger was not on the plaza. He was not anywhere in sight. A few of the more religious crossed themselves for fear that the Devil had walked in their midst. "Who was he?" one voice asked another. But Sarita, who was meekly listening to a lecture from Don Roméo on the propriety of dancing with strangers, did not have to ask. She had a strong suspicion that she had danced that night within the circling arm of Pepe Gonzalez.

TAKE NOTES

Everest *from* Touch the Top of the World

by Erik Weihenmayer

We left our tents a little before 9:00 P.M. on May 24. Because of our twenty-four-hour delay and the apprehension of other expeditions to share a summit day with me, we moved across the South Col with only one other team behind us. We had no worries of the typical horde clogging the fixed lines but could direct our full focus toward the mountain. The wind was blowing so loudly through the col that I couldn't hear the bells jingling from Chris's ice axe. Chris and I expected this, so for the first two hours he clanked his metal axe against rocks he passed. Finally, we worked our way around to the mountain's leeward[1] side, where Everest itself protected us from the wind. Chris had lost his voice, so his verbal directions were sparse. At each anchor, he'd hold the new line with his hand, so I could locate it and clip in. Chris was moving in front of me at his usual rock-solid pace, and I was right on his heels. We were making unbelievable time.

As we got higher up the mountain, four distinct changes had begun to work in my favor. Earlier, in the icefall, each step was very specific, but the terrain above the South Col consisted of steep forty-five-degree snow faces a hundred yards wide, intermingled with ten-to-fifty-foot crumbly rock steps. I could stay in the kicked boot holes of Chris or kick my own steps. Where I stepped had become less important than maintaining internal balance. I could breathe, scan my ice axe, and count on the next step. The slope was often so steep that I could lean forward and feel the rock or snow steps with my gloved hands, and I had trained myself long ago to save energy by landing my feet in the same holds my hands had just left. Finally, when I needed it most, the mountain had given me a pattern.

The thin oxygen of extreme altitude reduced us to a crawl. It was like moving through a bizarre atmosphere

---

1. **leeward** (lē′ wərd′) *adj.* away from the wind.

of syrup mixed with a narcotic. My team, struggling just to put one foot in front of the other, moved so slowly, it gave me more time to scan my axe across the snow and feel my way forward. The third equalizer was the darkness. With just a trickle of light produced by headlamps, my sighted team could only see a few feet in front of them. Bulky goggles blocked their side vision, and oxygen masks covered much of their visual field. Also, the pure oxygen trickling through their masks would flow up and freeze the lenses of their goggles so that they constantly had to remove them to wipe the lenses clean. Those brief moments when eyes are exposed to the elements, corneas will freeze, and the intense rays of the sun reflecting off the snow cause instant snow blindness. Not once did I ever have to worry about these complications.

In addition, my teammates had chosen smaller masks that rode low and tight across their cheeks and hung mostly below their chins. This allowed climbers to see better and prevented pure oxygen from seeping into their lenses, but also allowed plenty of pure oxygen to escape into the wind. I, on the other hand, had the luxury of choosing the largest mask I could find and wore it high on my face, getting the most benefit from the oxygen flow and the ambient air around the mask. I'm sure I made a freakish sight with my gigantic mask covering my goggles, like a day long ago in wrestling practice when I had put my sweatshirt on backward, with the hood covering my face, and chased the terrified freshmen around the mat. The consistent terrain, the altitude, the mask, and the darkness were great equalizers. I wouldn't go so far as to claim these gave me an advantage, but it was a matter of perspective. The mountain had gotten desperately harder for everyone else, while it had gotten slightly easier for me.

For two and a half months, all the decisions, the logistics, the backup safety plans had been implemented and executed by PV, and now, somewhere below the Balcony, the exhausting burden of leadership finally took its toll. Suddenly feeling listless and unable to catch his breath even with his oxygen bottle at full flow, PV had arduously turned back. He managed to convince Brad and Sherm, next to

TAKE NOTES

TAKE NOTES

him, that he was strong enough to descend alone, in retrospect, a ploy that might have turned deadly, but PV's weary brain had never stopped calculating the big picture. He had refused to divert any energy from the team's summit effort. Through periodic radio checks as PV dropped altitude, I could hear his characteristically hyper voice growing flat, and just below a steep ice bulge, only an hour from Camp Four, PV sat down in the snow.

"I'm very tired," he said. "I don't know if I can make it. I might need some assistance." PV's one warning before we left the tent was "If you sit down, you'll stay there." So, beginning to panic, I ripped my radio out of my pocket. "Is anyone near PV who can help him down?" I asked. "Is anyone reading me?" I repeated myself several times to empty static.

A few weeks earlier, Dr. Gipe had received the sad news that a close family friend had been killed in a skiing accident; a three-thousand-foot day in the Death Zone just didn't seem fair to his family, so that night, he had never left his tent. His decision was a tough one to make, but extremely fortunate for PV's sake. "This is Gipe at the South Col," finally came over the radio. "I'm strapping on my crampons right now. I'm going out to get PV." Dr. Gipe met PV about a half an hour from camp, up again and staggering slowly toward the tents.

With the first crisis of the night averted, Chris and I plodded up a steep gully, which led us to the Balcony, a flat snow platform, ten feet wide. Michael Brown arrived first at about 2:00 A.M., with Chris and me right behind. All night, the weather had remained clear, with high clouds to the southeast and distant lightning flashes illuminating the sky, but at the Balcony, our luck suddenly ran out. We walked into a blasting storm. Wind and horizontal snow raked our down suits and covered us with a layer of ice. The lightning strikes were now on top of us, exploding like a pyrotechnic[2] show. Chris later said he couldn't see his feet through the blowing snow, which stopped us short, since the southeast ridge above narrowed to

---

2. **pyrotechnic** (pī′ rə tek′ nik) *adj.* of or pertaining to fireworks; here, brilliant; dazzling.

fifteen feet wide. Mike O.'s and Didrik's headlamps had simultaneously flickered out, and one of Didrik's crampons had popped off. "Someone come and help us," Mike yelled over the radio. Charley headed back and found them sitting in the snow only twenty feet away.

Chris and I huddled together in the wind, waiting for the others to arrive. "What do you think, Big E?" he asked. "It's lookin' pretty grim." When the others trickled in, Sherm wanted to go on; Charley wanted to turn back, and Erie thought we should wait. For forty-five minutes, we waited, periodic arguments breaking out whether to go on or descend. I was beginning to shiver and forced myself to bounce up and down, and to windmill my arms. We were so close, and I was feeling strong. Turning back was a crushing proposition, but I also wasn't willing to go bullheadedly forward and throw my life away. My mind was starting to settle on the possibility of turning back, when Kevin's voice from Base Camp crackled over my radio. Throughout the expedition, Kevin had been learning to read the satellite weather reports we received every few days over the Internet. From the weather map, it appeared the storm was moving rapidly to the northeast toward Bhutan, and where we stood on the Balcony, we were directly northeast of Base Camp. "Hey you guys, don't quit yet," his voice sounded urgent. "The storm's cleared down here. It just might pass over you."

"Weather is also clearing here," Kami said from Camp Two below. Chris glanced over at me. Beyond my right hip, shining through the storm clouds, he could see a star. "Let's see if this thing breaks up," he said. Sherm must have felt good tidings, too, because he pushed on. Chris and I followed.

Following the narrow exposed southeast shoulder, I felt the first warmth of the sun about 4:00 A.M.; so high up, no other mountain blocked the sunrise. The weather had thankfully turned spectacular.

Still hours below the South Summit, we were stalled out again. The fixed lines, running up the steepest slope yet, had been frozen over by a hard windswept crust of snow. Jeff and Brad moved ahead, pulling the lines free, an exhausting job at twenty-eight thousand

TAKE NOTES

TAKE NOTES

feet. The job was quickly wearing Jeff down, but he said later that with each gasping breath as he heaved the rope free, he envisioned the two of us standing on top together. Soon he was beginning to feel faint and dizzy. As he knelt in the snow, Brad, behind him, examined his oxygen equipment and assessed that his regulator, connecting the long tube of his mask to his bottle, had malfunctioned. The internal valves responsible for regulating flow were notoriously prone to freezing shut. "Who's got an extra regulator?" Brad called out over the radio, but tired bodies and brains could not recall who had thrown in the extras in the presummit shuffle. "My day's finished if I can't find the extra," Jeff yelled testily.

It may not have been PV's time to summit, but he wasn't through benefiting the team. "Calm down," he advised, lying weakly on his back in his tent. "Everyone take a deep breath. Ang Pasang and Sherm are carrying the extra regulators." Luckily, Ang Pasang was only a hundred feet behind. Together, Brad and Ang Pasang screwed on Jeff's new regulator.

By 8:00 A.M., we had struggled on to the South Summit, 28,700 feet. After a short rest, Chris took off for the summit, cranking it into "Morris gear," and Luis took over in front of me. From the South Summit, the true summit is still at least two hours away across the three-hundred-foot-long knife-edge ridge, up the fifty-foot vertical Hillary Step, and finally traversing up a long slightly broader ridge to the summit.

Jeff, exhausted from his two-hour struggle pulling lines, stopped short in front of me. "I'm wasted. I've gotta go down," he said reluctantly. "This'll have to be my summit."

For a moment I wanted to goad him on the way we had done each other on winter training climbs of Colorado fourteeners. "If you wanna turn back, just say the word," we'd jab. "Of course, I'll have to tell everyone you were a whiney little crybaby." But 28,700 feet above sea level wasn't the place to motivate with bravado or ego, so assessing that he was strong enough to get down, I rested a hand on Jeff's shoulder and wished him a safe descent. Jeff had been with me from the beginning, practically introducing me to the mountains. He had shown extraordinary patience as I stumbled along experimenting with brand-new trekking poles. We had even stood together on the summit of Denali[3] and El Capitan,[4] so I knew that reaching the summit of Mt. Everest without him wouldn't feel complete. Suddenly, a wave of heavy exhaustion passed over me, and I felt weary and crumpled. "Maybe I'll go down too," I readied my lips to say, but then Luis was crunching through the snow in front of me, and I forced myself to revive.

Down-climbing the twenty-foot vertical snow face on the backside of the South Summit leading onto the knife-edge ridge went against my survival instinct. The ridge is the width of a picnic table and always heavily corniced[5] with snow. To the left is an eight-thousand-foot drop into Nepal, and on the right, a twelve-thousand-foot drop into Tibet. PV had told me that while crossing the ridge on his 1998 attempt, he had driven his ice axe into the snow and, after withdrawing it, had stared through the small hole into the early morning light of Tibet. In 1995, on Brad's second attempt, a climber in front of him had taken his first step onto the ridge just before the entire right half of it dropped away. The climber jumped back to safety, but a second later he would have ridden the cornice into Tibet. This year, the ridge was drier and more stable. Frozen boot steps traversed along the lefthand side. I'd scan my pole until it dropped into a boot mark, then cautiously lower my foot. I knew I couldn't make a mistake here: six hard steady breaths, another solid step, and a relaxed, focused mind like clear water.

Climbing the Hillary Step, I felt I was in my element, feeling the rock under my gloves. I stuck the crampon points of my right foot tenuously into a tiny crack and the left points into a cornice of snow, slid my ascender as high as it would go on the rope, and stood up and quickly reached for the next knob of rock. At the top, I awkwardly belly-flopped onto a flat ledge, slowly pulled myself to my feet, and began traversing the last slope to the summit. For forty minutes I trudged upward. My heavy sluggish muscles felt as if they were pushing

---

3. **Denali** (di nä´ lē) name of the National Park in which Mt. McKinley is located.
4. **El Capitan** (ol´ ka´ pē tan´) a peak In the Sierra Nevada mountain range in the Yosemite Valley of central California.
5. **corniced** (kôr´ nist) *adj.* in architecture, having a projecting decorative strip atop a wall or building; here, characterized by overhanging masses of snow or ice.

TAKE NOTES

TAKE NOTES

through wet cement. With each step closer, the real possibility of standing on top began to trickle through my focused brain. I had speculated success in a conceptual way and as a way to motivate myself when I was down, but it was dangerous to believe it as a fact. A team could be turned back for so many reasons at any time. Just keep moving, I thought. You're not there yet.

Then a body moved down the slope toward me and I felt thin wiry arms beneath a puffy down suit wrapping around me. "Big E!" The voice rasped, so hollow and wispy, I had trouble recognizing it as Chris. His voice tried to say more, but his quaking words dissipated in the wind. Then he leaned in against my ear. "Big E"—his voice gave way to tears, then struggled out in an immense effort—"you're about to stand on top of the world." Then he quickly let go and hurriedly moved down the slope.

Luis and I linked our arms, and in a few steps, the earth flattened and the massive sky closed around me on all sides. "This is Erik, Luis, and Ang Pasang," I said over the radio. "We're on the top. I can't believe it; we're on the top."

"You're the best, Big E!" Kevin yelled from Base Camp. "I love you guys." I could hear the entire Base Camp crew cheering behind him.

"You're the strongest man in the world," PV said.

I turned around, surprised to hear more crampons moving up behind me. "I wasn't gonna let you stand on top and hear about it the rest of my life," Jeff said, with a little pep left in his voice. One of the greatest joys of my summit was that Jeff hadn't turned back at all. From the South Summit, he had watched us down-climb onto the knife-edge ridge and move toward the Hillary Step. Later he told me, "I simply had to follow." Behind Jeff came Erie, Michael B., Didrik, Charley, and Mike O. Sherm had been the first on the team to summit, becoming the oldest man in history to stand on the top of the world, but better than his record was the fact that his son, Brad, had stepped onto the summit right behind him. Nineteen team members made it to the summit: eleven Westerners and eight Sherpas, the most from one team to reach the top in a single day. So it was a crowded summit as we all stood together, hugging and crying on a snow platform the size of a single-car garage.

Another storm was rolling in from the north. "Weather's changing fast," PV called up on the radio. "You guys need to go down immediately." I turned to head down with Erie, when Jeff said, "Wait a second, Big E. You'll only be here once in your life. Look around. Think about where you are and what you've done." So I suspended my nerves for a moment, reached down and touched the snow through my gloved hand, listened to the Sherpa prayer flags flapping in the wind, and heard the infinite sound of space around me, as on my first rock climb. After I had gone blind almost twenty years ago, I would have been proud to find the bathroom, so I said a quick prayer and thanked God for giving me so much. Then it was time to go down.

We descended through heavy snowfall but, thankfully, little wind. Erie took over guiding me, down the Hillary Step, across the knife edge, and contrary to his fears that he wouldn't be strong enough to make the top, he was stronger and more lucid on the way down from Everest's summit than most were on the top of a peak in Colorado. Reaching our tents at about 3:00 P.M., I hugged Erie. "Today," I said, "you were my guardian angel. I'm glad you're here."

That night, Kevin radioed up to report that he had called Ellie on the sat phone with the news. "She screamed loud enough to break the neighbors' windows." He laughed. The next days were exhausting as we fought our way through the screaming wind of the South Col, down the Lhotse Face—where my rubbery legs refused to obey my brain—and finally one last trip through the icefall. At the bottom, in Superman's Palace, of course, the whole team was waiting, and the party lasted long after the sun had sunk below Pumori.

Despite our success, plenty of detractors voiced their opinions on Internet chat rooms and in letters to the editor. I've heard all the ridiculous assumptions.

"Now that a blind guy's climbed it, everyone's going to want to climb it. They're going to think it's easy. People will probably get hurt."

TAKE NOTES

TAKE NOTES

"Why are people thinking this is such a big deal? Anyone can be short-roped to the top by nineteen seeing-eye guides."

My teammates constantly come to my rescue with carefully crafted comebacks like "Before you start spouting a bunch of lies over a public forum, get your facts straight, dude!"

"Don't let 'em get to you," Chris Morris said after I shared with him their comments. "You climbed every inch of that mountain, and then some."

I knew he was right. There were some who would never be convinced, others who still had no idea what to think, but many others for whom the climb forced a higher expectation of their own possibilities. I don't climb mountains to prove to anyone that blind people can do this or that. I climb for the same reason an artist paints a picture: because it brings me great joy. But I'd be lying if I didn't admit my secret satisfaction in facing those cynics and blowing through their doubts, destroying their negative stereotypes, taking their very narrow parameters of what's possible and what's not, and shattering them into a million pieces.

When those parameters are rebuilt, thousands and thousands of people will live with fewer barriers placed before them, and if my climbs can play a small role in opening doors of opportunity and hope for those who will come after us, then I am very proud of what we were able to achieve . . .

Keep Memory Alive

by Elie Wiesel

It is with a profound sense of humility that I accept the honor you have chosen to bestow upon me. I know: your choice transcends me. This both frightens and pleases me.

It frightens me because I wonder: do I have the right to represent the multitudes who have perished? Do I have the right to accept this great honor on their behalf? I do not. That would be presumptuous. No one may speak for the dead, no one may interpret their mutilated dreams and visions.

It pleases me because I may say that this honor belongs to all the survivors and their children, and through us, to the Jewish people with whose destiny I have always identified.

I remember: it happened yesterday or eternities ago. A young Jewish boy discovered the kingdom of night. I remember his bewilderment, I remember his anguish. It all happened so fast. The ghetto.[1] The deportation. The sealed cattle car. The fiery altar upon which the history of our people and the future of mankind were meant to be sacrificed.

I remember: he asked his father: "Can this be true? This is the 20th century, not the Middle Ages. Who would allow such crimes to be committed? How could the world remain silent?"

And now the boy is turning to me: "Tell me," he asks. "What have you done with my future? What have you done with your life?"

And I tell him that I have tried. That I have tried to keep memory alive, that I have tried to fight those who would forget. Because if we forget, we are guilty, we are accomplices.

And then I explained to him how naive we were, that the world did know and remain silent. And that is

---

1. The ghetto (getʹ ō) During the Second World War, the Nazis forced Jews in European cities to live in crowded, restricted neighborhoods, or ghettos.

TAKE NOTES

why I swore never to be silent whenever and wherever human beings endure suffering and humiliation. We must always take sides. Neutrality[2] helps the oppressor, never the victim. Silence encourages the tormentor, never the tormented.

---

2. **Neutrality** (n$\overline{oo}$ tral′ ə tē) *n.* state of not taking sides in a conflict; quality of being unbiased.

The American Idea

by Theodore H. White

TAKE NOTES

The idea was there at the very beginning, well before Thomas Jefferson put it into words—and the idea rang the call.

Jefferson himself could not have imagined the reach of his call across the world in time to come when he wrote:

"We hold these truths to be self-evident, that all men are created equal, that they are endowed by their Creator with certain unalienable rights, that among these are life, liberty, and the pursuit of happiness."

But over the next two centuries the call would reach the potato patches of Ireland, the ghettoes of Europe, the paddyfields of China, stirring farmers to leave their lands and townsmen their trades and thus unsettling all traditional civilizations.

It is the call from Thomas Jefferson, embodied in the great statue that looks down the Narrows of New York Harbor,[1] and in the immigrants who answered the call, that we now celebrate.

Some of the first European Americans had come to the new continent to worship God in their own way, others to seek their fortunes. But, over a century-and-a-half, the new world changed those Europeans, above all the Englishmen who had come to North America. Neither King nor Court nor Church could stretch over the ocean to the wild continent. To survive, the first emigrants had to learn to govern themselves. But the freedom of the wilderness whetted their appetites for more freedoms. By the time Jefferson drafted his call, men were in the field fighting for those new-learned freedoms, killing and being killed by English soldiers, the best-trained troops in the world, supplied by the world's greatest navy. Only something worth dying for could unite American volunteers and keep them in the field—a stated cause, a flag, a nation they could call their own.

---

1. **the great statue that looks down the Narrows of New York Harbor** Statue of Liberty.

When, on the Fourth of July, 1776, the colonial leaders who had been meeting as a Continental Congress in Philadelphia voted to approve Jefferson's Declaration of Independence, it was not puffed-up rhetoric for them to pledge to each other "our lives, our fortunes and our sacred honor." Unless their new "United States of America" won the war, the Congressmen would be judged traitors as relentlessly as would the irregulars-under-arms in the field. . . .

The new Americans were tough men fighting for a very tough idea. How they won their battles is a story for the schoolbooks, studied by scholars, wrapped in myths by historians and poets. But what is most important is the story of the idea that made them into a nation, the idea that had an explosive power undreamed of in 1776.

All other nations had come into being among people whose families had lived for time out of mind on the same land where they were born. Englishmen are English, Frenchmen are French, Chinese are Chinese, while their governments come and go; their national states can be torn apart and remade without losing their nationhood. But Americans are a nation born of an idea; not the place, but the idea, created the United States Government.

The story we celebrate . . . is the story of how this idea worked itself out, how it stretched and changed and how the call for "life, liberty and the pursuit of happiness" does still, as it did in the beginning, mean different things to different people. •

The debate began with the drafting of the Declaration of Independence. That task was left to Jefferson of Virginia, who spent two weeks in an upstairs room in a Philadelphia boarding house penning a draft, while John Adams and Benjamin Franklin questioned, edited, hardened his phrases. By the end of that hot and muggy June, the three had reached agreement: the Declaration contained the ringing universal theme Jefferson strove for and, at the same time, voiced American grievances toughly enough to please the feisty Adams and the pragmatic Franklin. After brief debate, Congress passed it.

As the years wore on, the great debate expanded between Jefferson and Adams. The young nation flourished and Jefferson chose to think of America's promise as a call to all the world, its promises universal. A few weeks before he died, he wrote, "May it be to the world, what I believe it will be (to some parts sooner, to others later, but finally to all), the signal of arousing men to burst their chains." To Adams, the call meant something else—it was the call for American independence, the cornerstone of an American state.

Their argument ran through their successive Administrations. Adams, the second President, suspected the French Revolutionaries; Alien and Sedition Acts[2] were passed during his term of office to protect the American state and its liberties against French subversion. But Jefferson, the third President, welcomed the French. The two men, once close friends, became archrivals. Still, as they grew old, their rivalry faded; there was glory enough to share in what they had made; in 1812, they began a correspondence that has since become classic, remembering and taking comfort in the triumphs of their youth.

Adams and Jefferson lived long lives and died on the same day—the Fourth of July, 1826, 50 years to the day from the Continental Congress's approval of the Declaration. Legend has it that Adams breathed on his death bed, "Thomas Jefferson still survives." As couriers set out from Braintree[3] carrying the news of Adams's death, couriers were riding north from Virginia with the news of Jefferson's death. The couriers met in Philadelphia. Horace Greeley,[4] then a youth in Vermont, later remembered: ". . . When we learned . . . that Thomas Jefferson and John Adams, the author and the great champion, respectively, of the Declaration, had both died on that day, and that the messengers bearing South and North, respectively, the tidings of their decease, had met in Philadelphia, under the shadow of that Hall in which our independence was declared, it seemed that a Divine attestation had solemnly hallowed and sanctified the great anniversary by the impressive ministration of Death."

---

2. **Alien and Sedition Acts** laws passed by Congress in 1798 restricting immigration and regulating the expression of criticism of the government.
3. **Braintree** town in Massachusetts (now called Quincy) where John Adams lived and died.
4. **Horace Greeley** famous American newspaper publisher.

TAKE NOTES

How to React to Familiar Faces

by Umberto Eco

A few months ago, as I was strolling in New York, I saw, at a distance, a man I knew very well heading in my direction. The trouble was that I couldn't remember his name or where I had met him. This is one of those sensations you encounter especially when, in a foreign city, you run into someone you met back home, or vice versa. A face out of context creates confusion. Still, that face was so familiar that, I felt, I should certainly stop, greet him, converse; perhaps he would immediately respond, "My dear Umberto, how are you?" or "Were you able to do that thing you were telling me about?" And I would be at a total loss. It was too late to flee. He was still looking at the opposite side of the street, but now he was beginning to turn his eyes towards me. I might as well make the first move; I would wave and then, from his voice, his first remarks, I would try to guess his identity.

We were now only a few feet from each other, I was just about to break into a broad, radiant smile, when suddenly I recognized him. It was Anthony Quinn.[1] Naturally, I had never met him in my life, nor he me. In a thousandth of a second I was able to check myself, and I walked past him, my eyes staring into space.

Afterwards, reflecting on this incident, I realized how totally normal it was. Once before, in a restaurant, I had glimpsed Charlton Heston[2] and had felt an impulse to say hello. These faces inhabit our memory; watching the screen, we spend so many hours with them that they are as familiar to us as our relatives', even more so. You can be a student of mass communication, debate the effects of reality, or the confusion between the real and the imagined, and expound the way some people fall permanently into

---

1. **Anthony Quinn** (1915–2001) was a film actor who won two Academy Awards.
2. **Charlton Heston** (1923–2008) was a film actor who won an Academy Award for his role in the film Ben-Hur.

this confusion; but still you are not immune to the syndrome.[3] And there is worse.

I have received confidences from people who, appearing fairly frequently on TV, have been subjected to the mass media over a certain period of time. I'm not talking about Johnny Carson[4] or Oprah Winfrey, but public figures, experts who have participated in panel discussions often enough to become recognizable. All of them complain of the same disagreeable experience. Now, as a rule, when we see someone we don't know personally, we don't stare into his or her face at length, we don't point out the person to the friend at our side, we don't speak of this person in a loud voice when he or she can overhear. Such behavior would be rude, even—if carried too far—aggressive. But the same people who would never point to a customer at a counter and remark to a friend that the man is wearing a smart[5] tie behave quite differently with famous faces.

My guinea pigs[6] insist that, at a newsstand, in the tobacconist's, as they are boarding a train or entering a restaurant toilet, they encounter others who, among themselves, say aloud, "Look there's X." "Are you sure?" "Of course I'm sure. It's X, I tell you." And they continue their conversation amiably, while X hears them, and they don't care if he hears them: it's as if he didn't exist.

Such people are confused by the fact that a protagonist of the mass media's imaginary world should abruptly enter real life, but at the same time they behave in the presence of the real person as if he still belonged to the world of images, as if he were on a screen, or in a weekly picture magazine. As if they were speaking in his absence.

I might as well have grabbed Anthony Quinn by the lapel, dragged him to a phone booth, and called a friend to say, "Talk about coincidence! I've run into Anthony Quinn. And you know something? He seems

---

3. **syndrome** (sin′ drōm′) *n.* set of symptoms or characteristics occurring together and defining a disease or condition.
4. **Johnny Carson** (1925–2005) was the host of the nighttime talk show *The Tonight Show* for thirty years.
5. **smart** *adj.* stylish; fashionable.
6. **guinea** (gin′ ē) **pigs** subjects of an experiment (so-called because of the use of guinea pigs in laboratory experiments).

TAKE NOTES

real!" (After which I would throw Quinn aside and go on about my business.)

The mass media first convinced us that the imaginary was real, and now they are convincing us that the real is imaginary; and the more reality the TV screen shows us, the more cinematic[7] our everyday world becomes.

---

7. cinematic (sin′ ə mat′ ik) *adj.* of or like movies.

The Poetic Interpretation of the Twist

by Cornelius Eady

I know what you're expecting to hear.
You think to yourself: Here's a guy who must
    understand what the twist was all about.
Look at the knuckles of his hands,
Look at his plain, blue shirt hanging out of the
    back of his trousers.
5 The twist must have been the equivalent of
    the high sign
In a secret cult.

I know
I know
I know

10 But listen: I am still confused by the mini-skirt
As well as the deep meaning of vinyl on everything.
The twist was just a children's game to us.
I know you expect there ought to be more to this,
The reason the whole world decided to uncouple,

15 But why should I lie to you? Let me pull up a chair
And in as few words as possible,
Re-create my sister,
Who was renowned for running like a giraffe.
Let me re-create my neighborhood,

20 A dead-end street next to the railroad tracks.
Let me re-create
My father, who would escape the house by bicycle
And do all the grocery shopping by himself.

Let's not forget the pool hall and the barbershop,

25 Each with their strange flavors of men,
And while we're on the subject,
I must not slight the ragweed,
The true rose of the street.

TAKE NOTES

All this will still not give you the twist.
30 Forgive me for running on like this.
Your question has set an expectation
That is impossible to meet

Your question has put on my shoulders
A troublesome responsibility

35 Because the twist is gone.
It is the foundation of a bridge
That has made way for a housing project

And I am sorry to admit
You have come to the wrong person.
40 I recall the twist
The way we recall meeting a distant aunt as a baby
Or the afternoons spent in homeroom
Waiting for the last bell.

My head hurts.
45 I am tired of remembering.
Perhaps you can refresh my memory
And tell me
How we got on this topic?
As a favor to me,
50 Let's not talk anymore about old dances.

I have an entire world on the tip of my tongue.

The Empty Dance Shoes

by Cornelius Eady

My friends,
As it has been proven in the laboratory,
An empty pair of dance shoes
Will sit on the floor like a wart
5 Until it is given a reason to move.

Those of us who study inertia
(Those of us covered with wild hair and sleep)
Can state this without fear:
The energy in a pair of shoes at rest
10 Is about the same as that of a clown

Knocked flat by a sandbag.
This you can tell your friends with certainty:
A clown, flat on his back,
Is a lot like an empty pair of
15   dancing shoes.

An empty pair of dancing shoes
Is also a lot like a leaf
Pressed in a book.
And now you know a simple truth:
20 A leaf pressed in, say, *The Colossus*
          by Sylvia Plath,[1]
Is no different from an empty pair of dance shoes

Even if those shoes are in the middle of the
          Stardust Ballroom
With all the lights on, and hot music shakes the
          windows
25   up and down the block.
This is the secret of inertia:
The shoes run on their own sense of the world.
They are in sympathy with the rock the kid skips
          over the lake
30 After it settles to the mud.
Not with the ripples,
But with the rock.

TAKE NOTES

A practical and personal application of inertia
Can be found in the question:
35 Whose Turn Is It
To Take Out The Garbage?
An empty pair of dance shoes
Is a lot like the answer to this question,
As well as book-length poems
40 Set in the Midwest.

To sum up:
An empty pair of dance shoes
Is a lot like the sand the 98-pound weakling
        brushes from his cheeks
45 As the bully tows away his girlfriend.
Later,

When he spies the coupon at the back of the comic
        book,
He is about to act upon a different set of scientific
        principles.
He is ready to dance.

---

1. *The Colossus* **by Sylvia Plath** volume of poetry by American poet Sylvia Plath
   (1932–1963).

The Bridegroom

by Alexander Pushkin

translated by D.M. Thomas

For three days Natasha,
The merchant's daughter,
Was missing. The third night,
She ran in, distraught.
5 Her father and mother
Plied her with questions.
She did not hear them,
She could hardly breathe.

Stricken with foreboding
10 They pleaded, got angry,
But still she was silent;
At last they gave up.
Natasha's cheeks regained
Their rosy color.
15 And cheerfully again
She sat with her sisters.

Once at the shingle-gate
She sat with her friends
—And a swift troika[1]
20 Flashed by before them;
A handsome young man
Stood driving the horses;
Snow and mud went flying,
Splashing the girls.

25 He gazed as he flew past,
And Natasha gazed.
He flew on. Natasha froze.
Headlong she ran home.
"It was he! It was he!"
30 She cried. "I know it!
I recognized him! Papa,
Mama, save me from him!"

Full of grief and fear,
They shake their heads, sighing.

---

1. troika (troi′ kə) *n.* Russian carriage or sleigh drawn by a team of three horses.

TAKE NOTES

TAKE NOTES

35 Her father says: "My child,
Tell me everything.
If someone has harmed you,
Tell us . . . even a hint."
She weeps again and
40 Her lips remain sealed. •

The next morning, the old
Matchmaking woman
Unexpectedly calls and
Sings the girl's praises;
45 Says to the father: "You
Have the goods and I
A buyer for them:
A handsome young man.

"He bows low to no one,
50 He lives like a lord
With no debts nor worries;
He's rich and he's generous,
Says he will give his bride,
On their wedding-day,
55 A fox-fur coat, a pearl,
Gold rings, brocaded[2] dresses,

"Yesterday, out driving,
He saw your Natasha;
Shall we shake hands
60 And get her to church?"
The woman starts to eat
A pie, and talks in riddles,
While the poor girl
Does not know where to look.

65 "Agreed," says her father;
"Go in happiness
To the altar, Natasha;
It's dull for you here;
A swallow should not spend
70 All its time singing,
It's time for you to build
A nest for your children."

Natasha leaned against
The wall and tried

---

2. **brocaded** (brō kād′ əd) *adj.* with raised designs woven into the cloth.

75 To speak—but found herself
   Sobbing; she was shuddering
   And laughing. The matchmaker
   Poured out a cup of water,
   Gave her some to drink,
80 Splashed some in her face.

   Her parents are distressed.
   Then Natasha recovered,
   And calmly she said:
   "Your will be done. Call
85 My bridegroom to the feast,
   Bake loaves for the whole world,
   Brew sweet mead[3] and call
   The law to the feast."

   "Of course, Natasha, angel!
90 You know we'd give our lives
   To make you happy!"
   They bake and they brew;
   The worthy guests come,
   The bride is led to the feast,
95 Her maids sing and weep;
   Then horses and a sledge[4]

   With the groom—and all sit.
   The glasses ring and clatter,
   The toasting-cup is passed
100 From hand to hand in tumult,
   The guests are drunk. •

   BRIDEGROOM
   "Friends, why is my fair bride
   Sad, why is she not
   Feasting and serving?"

105 The bride answers the groom:
   "I will tell you why
   As best I can. My soul
   Knows no rest, day and night
   I weep; an evil dream
110 Oppresses me." Her father
   Says: "My dear child, tell us
   What your dream is."

---

3. mead (mēd) *n.* drink made of fermented honey and water.
4. sledge (slej) *n.* sleigh.

TAKE NOTES

"I dreamed," she says, "that I
Went into a forest,
115 It was late and dark;
The moon was faintly
Shining behind a cloud;
I strayed from the path;
Nothing stirred except
120 The tops of the pine-trees.

"And suddenly, as if
I was awake, I saw
A hut. I approach the hut
And knock at the door
125 —Silence. A prayer on my lips
I open the door and enter.
A candle burns. All
Is silver and gold."

BRIDEGROOM
"What is bad about that?
130 It promises wealth."

BRIDE
"Wait, sir, I've not finished.
Silently I gazed
On the silver and gold,
The cloths, the rugs, the silks
135 From Novgorod,[5] and I
Was lost in wonder.

"Then I heard a shout
And a clatter of hoofs . . .
Someone has driven up
140 To the porch. Quickly
I slammed the door and hid
Behind the stove. Now
I hear many voices . . .
Twelve young men come in,

145 "And with them is a girl,
Pure and beautiful.
They've taken no notice
Of the ikons,[6] they sit
To the table without

---

5. **Novgorod** (näv′ gə räd′) city in northwestern Russia.
6. **ikons** (ī′ känz′) *n.* sacred religious images.

150 Praying or taking off
Their hats. At the head,
The eldest brother,

At his right, the youngest;
At his left, the girl.
155 Shouts, laughs, drunken clamor . . . "

BRIDEGROOM
"That betokens merriment."

BRIDE
"Wait, sir, I've not finished.
The drunken din goes on
And grows louder still.
160 Only the girl is sad.

"She sits silent, neither
Eating nor drinking;
But sheds tears in plenty;
The eldest brother
165 Takes his knife and, whistling,
Sharpens it; seizing her by
The hair he kills her
And cuts off her right hand."

"Why," says the groom, "this
170 Is nonsense! Believe me,
My love, your dream is not evil."
She looks him in the eyes.
"And from whose hand
Does this ring come?"
175 The bride said. The whole throng
Rose in the silence.

With a clatter the ring
Falls, and rolls along
The floor. The groom blanches,
180 Trembles. Confusion . . .
"Seize him!" the law commands.
He's bound, judged, put to death.
Natasha is famous!
Our song at an end.

TAKE NOTES

Making a Fist

by Naomi Shihab Nye

For the first time, on the road north of Tampico,[1]
I felt the life sliding out of me,
a drum in the desert, harder and harder to hear.
I was seven, I lay in the car
5 watching palm trees swirl a sickening pattern
     past the glass.
My stomach was a melon split wide inside my skin.

"How do you know if you are going to die?"
I begged my mother.
We had been traveling for days.
10 With strange confidence she answered,
"When you can no longer make a fist."

Years later I smile to think of that journey,
the borders we must cross separately,
stamped with our unanswerable woes.
15 I who did not die, who am still living,
still lying in the backseat behind all my questions,
clenching and opening one small hand.

---

1. **Tampico** (täm pē′ kō) seaport in eastern Mexico.

The Fish

by Elizabeth Bishop

TAKE NOTES

I caught a tremendous fish
and held him beside the boat
half out of water, with my hook
fast in a corner of his mouth.
5　He didn't fight.
He hadn't fought at all.
He hung a grunting weight,
battered and venerable
and homely. Here and there
10　his brown skin hung in strips
like ancient wallpaper,
and its pattern of darker brown
was like wallpaper:
shapes like full-blown roses
15　stained and lost through age.
He was speckled with barnacles,
fine rosettes of lime,
and infested
with tiny white sea-lice,
20　and underneath two or three
rags of green weed hung down.
While his gills were breathing in
the terrible oxygen
—the frightening gills,
25　fresh and crisp with blood,
that can cut so badly—
I thought of the coarse white flesh
packed in like feathers,
the big bones and the little bones,
30　the dramatic reds and blacks
of his shiny entrails,
and the pink swim-bladder
like a big peony.
I looked into his eyes
35　which were far larger than mine
but shallower, and yellowed,

TAKE NOTES

the irises backed and packed
with tarnished tinfoil
seen through the lenses
40 of old scratched isinglass.[1]
They shifted a little, but not
to return my stare.
—It was more like the tipping
of an object toward the light.
45 I admired his sullen face,
the mechanism of his jaw,
and then I saw
that from his lower lip
—if you could call it a lip—
50 grim, wet, and weaponlike,
hung five old pieces of fish-line,
or four and a wire leader
with the swivel still attached,
with all their five big hooks
55 grown firmly in his mouth.
A green line, frayed at the end
where he broke it, two heavier lines,
and a fine black thread
still crimped from the strain and snap
60 when it broke and he got away.
Like medals with their ribbons
frayed and wavering,
a five-haired beard of wisdom
trailing from his aching jaw.
65 I stared and stared
and victory filled up
the little rented boat,
from the pool of bilge
where oil had spread a rainbow
70 around the rusted engine
to the bailer rusted orange,
the sun-cracked thwarts[2]
the oarlocks on their strings,
the gunnels[3]—until everything
75 was rainbow, rainbow, rainbow!
And I let the fish go.

---

1. **isinglass** (ī´ zin glas´) *n.* transparent material once used in windows.
2. **thwarts** (thwôrts) *n.* seats in a boat for rowers.
3. **gunnels** (gun´ əlz) *n.* upper edges of the sides of a ship or boat.

The Guitar

by Federico García Lorca
translated by Elizabeth du Gué Trapier

Now begins the cry
Of the guitar,
Breaking the vaults
Of dawn.
5   Now begins the cry
Of the guitar.
Useless
To still it.
Impossible
10 To still it.
It weeps monotonously
As weeps the water,
As weeps the wind
Over snow.
15 Impossible
To still it.
It weeps
For distant things,
Warm southern sands
20 Desiring white camellias.
It mourns the arrow without a target,
The evening without morning.
And the first bird dead
Upon a branch.
25 O guitar!
A wounded heart,
Wounded by five swords.

Do Not Go Gentle into That Good Night

by Dylan Thomas

Do not go gentle into that good night,
Old age should burn and rave at close of day;
Rage, rage against the dying of the light.

Though wise men at their end know dark is right,
5   Because their words had forked no lightning they
Do not go gentle into that good night.

Good men, the last wave by, crying how bright
Their frail deeds might have danced in a green bay,
Rage, rage against the dying of the light.

10   Wild men who caught and sang the sun in flight,
And learn, too late, they grieved it on its way,
Do not go gentle into that good night.

Grave men, near death, who see with blinding sight
Blind eyes could blaze like meteors and be gay,
15   Rage, rage against the dying of the light.

And you, my father, there on the sad height,
Curse, bless, me now with your fierce tears, I pray.
Do not go gentle into that good night.
Rage, rage against the dying of the light.

Tanka

One cannot ask loneliness
How or where it starts.
On the cypress-mountain,[1]
Autumn evening.
    — Priest Jakuren
    translated by Geoffrey Bownas

Was it that I went to sleep
Thinking of him,
That he came in my dreams?
Had I known it a dream
I should not have wakened.
    — Ono Komachi
    translated by Geoffrey Bownas

---

1. **cypress-mountain** Cypress trees are cone-bearing evergreen trees native to North America, Europe, and Asia.

My City

by James Weldon Johnson

When I come down to sleep death's endless night,
    The threshold of the unknown dark to cross,
    What to me then will be the keenest loss,
When this bright world blurs on my fading sight?
5 Will it be that no more I shall see the trees
    Or smell the flowers or hear the singing birds
    Or watch the flashing streams or patient herds?
No, I am sure it will be none of these.
But, ah! Manhattan's sights and sounds, her smells,
10 Her crowds, her throbbing force, the thrill that
    comes
    From being of her a part, her subtile spells,
    Her shining towers, her avenues, her slums—
    O God! the stark, unutterable pity,
To be dead, and never again behold my city!

Sonnet 18

by William Shakespeare

Shall I compare thee to a summer's day?
Thou art more lovely and more temperate:
Rough winds do shake the darling buds of May,
And summer's lease hath all too short a date:
5   Sometime too hot the eye of heaven shines,
And often is his gold complexion dimmed;
And every fair from fair sometime declines,
By chance or nature's changing course untrimmed;[1]
But thy eternal summer shall not fade,
10   Nor lose possession of that fair thou owest;[2]
Nor shall Death brag thou wander'st in his shade,
When in eternal lines to time thou grow'st:
    So long as men can breathe, or eyes can see,
    So long lives this, and this gives life to thee.

---

1. **untrimmed** *adj.* stripped of ornaments or beautiful features.
2. **owest** (ō´ ist) *v.* own.

The Wind—tapped like a tired Man

by Emily Dickinson

> The Wind—tapped like a tired Man—
> And like a Host—"Come in"
> I boldly answered—entered then
> My Residence within
>
> 5 A Rapid—footless Guest—
> To offer whom a Chair
> Were as impossible as hand
> A Sofa to the Air—
>
> No Bone had He to bind Him—
> 10 His Speech was like the Push
> Of numerous Humming Birds at once
> From a superior Bush—
>
> His Countenance—a Billow—
> His Fingers, as He passed
> 15 Let go a music—as of tunes
> Blown tremulous in Glass—
>
> He visited—still flitting—
> Then like a timid Man
> Again, He tapped—'twas flurriedly—
> 20 And I became alone—

Glory

by Yusef Komunyakaa

Most were married teenagers
Working knockout shifts daybreak
To sunset six days a week—
Already old men playing ball
5   In a field between a row of shotgun houses
& the Magazine Lumber Company.
They were all Jackie Robinson
& Willie Mays, a touch of
Josh Gibson & Satchell Paige[1]
10   In each stance & swing, a promise
Like a hesitation pitch always
At the edge of their lives,
Arms sharp as rifles.
The Sunday afternoon heat
15   Flared like thin flowered skirts
As children & wives cheered.
The men were like cats
Running backwards to snag
Pop-ups & high-flies off
20   Fences, stealing each other's glory.
The old deacons & raconteurs[2]
Who umpired made an *Out* or *Safe*
Into a song & dance routine.
Runners hit the dirt
25   & slid into homeplate,
Cleats catching light,
As they conjured escapes, outfoxing
Double plays. In the few seconds
It took a man to eye a woman
30   Upon the makeshift bleachers,
A stolen base or homerun
Would help another man
Survive the new week.

---

1. **Jackie Robinson / & Willie Mays . . . / Josh Gibson & Satchell Paige** African American baseball stars of the 1920s through the 1970s.
2. **deacons & raconteurs** (rak′ än tʉrz′) assistant officers of a church and skilled storytellers.

TAKE NOTES

Metaphor

by Eve Merriam

Morning is
a new sheet of paper
for you to write on.

Whatever you want to say,
5 all day,
until night
folds it up
and files it away.

The bright words and the dark words
10 are gone
until dawn
and a new day
to write on.

Pride

by Dahlia Ravikovitch

translated by Chana Bloch and Ariel Bloch

I tell you, even rocks crack,
and not because of age.
For years they lie on their backs
in the heat and the cold,
5 so many years,
it almost seems peaceful.
They don't move, so the cracks stay hidden.
A kind of pride.
Years pass over them, waiting.
10 Whoever is going to shatter them
hasn't come yet.
And so the moss flourishes, the seaweed
whips around,
the sea pushes through and rolls back—
15 the rocks seem motionless.
Till a little seal comes to rub against them,
comes and goes away.
And suddenly the rock has an open wound.
I told you, when rocks break, it happens by surprise.
20 And people, too.

Jazz Fantasia

Carl Sandburg

Drum on your drums, batter on your banjoes,
sob on the long cool winding saxophones.
Go to it, O jazzmen.

Sling your knuckles on the bottoms of the happy
5 tin pans, let your trombones ooze, and go husha-
husha-hush with the slippery sand-paper.

Moan like an autumn wind high in the lonesome
   treetops,
moan soft like you wanted somebody terrible, cry
   like a
racing car slipping away from a motorcycle cop,
10 bang-bang! you jazzmen, bang altogether drums,
   traps,
banjoes, horns, tin cans—
make two people fight on the
top of a stairway and scratch each other's eyes in a
clinch[1] tumbling down the stairs.

Can[2] the rough stuff ... now a Mississippi steamboat
15 pushes up the night river with a hoo-hoo-hoo-oo . . .
   and
the green lanterns calling to the high soft stars . . .
   a red
moon rides on the humps of the low river hills . . .
   go to it,
O jazzmen.

---

1. **clinch** *n.* in boxing, the act of gripping the opponent's body with the arms.
2. **Can** *v.* slang for "stop" or "cease."

Meeting at Night

by Robert Browning

1

The gray sea and the long black land;
And the yellow half-moon large and low;
And the startled little waves that leap
In fiery ringlets from their sleep,
5 As I gain the cove with pushing prow,
And quench its speed i' the slushy sand.

2

Then a mile of warm sea-scented beach;
Three fields to cross till a farm appears;
A tap at the pane, the quick sharp scratch
10 And blue spurt of a lighted match,
And a voice less loud, through its joys and fears,
Than the two hearts beating each to each!

TAKE NOTES

Reapers

by Jean Toomer

Black reapers with the sound of steel on stones
Are sharpening scythes. I see them place the hones[1]
In their hip-pockets as a thing that's done,
And start their silent swinging, one by one.
5 Black horses drive a mower through the weeds,
And there, a field rat, startled, squealing bleeds,
His belly close to ground. I see the blade,
Blood-stained, continue cutting weeds and shade.

---

1. scythes (sīth*z*) **. . . hones** A scythe is a tool for cutting grain or grass, consisting of a sharp blade attached to a long handle. A hone is a hard stone used to sharpen a metal blade.

The Weary Blues

by Langston Hughes

Droning a drowsy syncopated[1] tune,
Rocking back and forth to a mellow croon,
    I heard a Negro play.
Down on Lenox Avenue[2] the other night
5 By the pale dull pallor of an old gas light
    He did a lazy sway. . . .
    He did a lazy sway. . . .
To the tune o' those Weary Blues.
With his ebony hands on each ivory key
10 He made that poor piano moan with melody.
    O Blues!
Swaying to and fro on his rickety stool
He played that sad raggy tune like a musical fool.
    Sweet Blues!
15 Coming from a black man's soul.
    O Blues!
In a deep song voice with a melancholy tone
I heard that Negro sing, that old piano moan—
    "Ain't got nobody in all this world,
20   Ain't got nobody but ma self.
    I's gwine to quit ma frownin'
    And put ma troubles on the shelf."
Thump, thump, thump, went his foot on the floor.
He played a few chords then he sang some more—
25   "I got the Weary Blues
    And I can't be satisfied.
    Got the Weary Blues
    And can't be satisfied—
    I ain't happy no mo'
30   And I wish that I had died."
And far into the night he crooned that tune.
The stars went out and so did the moon.
The singer stopped playing and went to bed
While the Weary Blues echoed through his head.
35 He slept like a rock or a man that's dead.

---

1. **syncopated** (sin′ kə pāt′ id) *adj.* with a catchy or an emphatic rhythm created by accenting beats that are usually unaccented.
2. **Lenox Avenue** street in Harlem, a historic African American neighborhood in New York City.

A Tree Telling Of Orpheus

by Denise Levertov

TAKE NOTES

White dawn. Stillness.　　When the rippling began
　　I took it for sea-wind, coming to our valley with
　　　rumors
　　of salt, of treeless horizons. But the white fog
　　didn't stir; the leaves of my brothers remained
　　　outstretched,
5　unmoving.
　　　　　Yet the rippling drew nearer—and then
　　my own outermost branches began to tingle,
　　　almost as if
　　fire had been lit below them, too close, and their
　　　twig-tips
　　were drying and curling.
10　　　　　　　　　　Yet I was not afraid, only
　　　　　　　　　deeply alert.
　　I was the first to see him, for I grew
　　　out on the pasture slope, beyond the forest.
　　He was a man, it seemed: the two
15　moving stems, the short trunk, the two
　　arm-branches, flexible, each with five leafless
　　　　　　　　　　　　twigs at their ends,
　　and the head that's crowned by brown or gold grass,
　　bearing a face not like the beaked face of a bird,
20　　　　　more like a flower's.
　　　　　　　　　　He carried a burden made of
　　some cut branch bent while it was green,
　　strands of a vine tight-stretched across it. From this,
　　when he touched it, and from his voice
25　which unlike the wind's voice had no need of our
　　leaves and branches to complete its sound,
　　　　　　　　　　　came the ripple,
　　But it was now no longer a ripple (he had come
　　near and stopped in my first shadow) it was a wave
　　　that bathed me
30　　　　　as if rain
　　　　　　　rose from below and around me

instead of falling.
And what I felt was no longer a dry tingling:

      I seemed to be singing as he sang, I seemed
        to know
35   what the lark knows; all my sap
        was mounting towards the sun that by now
         had risen, the mist was rising, the grass
was drying, yet my roots felt music moisten them
deep under earth.
40   He came still closer, leaned on my trunk:
        the bark thrilled like a leaf still-folded.
Music! There was no twig of me not
          trembling with joy and fear.

Then as he sang
45 it was no longer sounds only that made the music:
he spoke, and as no tree listens I listened, and
    language
       came into my roots
           out of the earth,
     into my bark
50   out of the air,
     into the pores of my greenest shoots
      gently as dew
and there was no word he sang but I knew its
    meaning.
He told of journeys,
55   of where sun and moon go while we stand in
      dark,
    of an earth-journey he dreamed he would take
      some day
deeper than roots . . .
He told of the dreams of man, wars, passions, griefs,
     and I, a tree, understood words—ah, it seemed
60 my thick bark would split like a sapling's that
         grew too fast in the spring
when a late frost wounds it.

         Fire he sang,
that trees fear, and I, a tree, rejoiced in its flames.
65 New buds broke forth from me though it was full
    summer.
    As though his lyre (now I knew its name)
    were both frost and fire, its chords flamed

TAKE NOTES

____

up to the crown of me.
        I was seed again.
70   I was fern in the swamp.
           I was coal.
And at the heart of my wood
(so close I was to becoming man or a god)
    there was a kind of silence, a kind of sickness,
75   something akin to what men call boredom,
                     something

(the poem descended a scale, a stream over stones)
         that gives to a candle a coldness
            in the midst of its burning, he said.

80 It was then,
       when in the blaze of his power that
             reached me and changed me
    I thought I should fall my length,
that the singer began
85   to leave me.   Slowly
       moved from my noon shadow
                to open light,
words leaping and dancing over his shoulders
back to me
90   rivery sweep of lyre-tones becoming
slowly again
          ripple.
And I
       in terror
95   but not in doubt of
              what I must do
in anguish, in haste,
       wrenched from the earth root after root,
the soil heaving and cracking, the moss tearing
   asunder—
100 and behind me the others: my brothers
forgotten since dawn. In the forest
they too had heard,
and were pulling their roots in pain
out of a thousand years' layers of dead leaves,
105   rolling the rocks away,
           breaking themselves
             out of
           their depths.

You would have thought we would lose the sound
        of the lyre,
110   of the singing
so dreadful the storm-sounds were, where there
        was no storm,
                        no wind but the rush of our
branches moving, our trunks breasting the air.
        But the music!
115   The music reached us.

Clumsily,
        stumbling over our own roots,
                                rustling our leaves
                                        in answer,
120 we moved, we followed.
All day we followed, up hill and down.
                                We learned to dance,
for he would stop, where the ground was flat,
                                and words he said
125 taught us to leap and to wind in and out
around one another   in figures   the lyre's
        measure designed.
The singer
        laughed till he wept to see us, he was so glad.
                                        At sunset
130 we came to this place I stand in, this knoll[1]
with its ancient grove that was bare grass then.
        In the last light of the day his song became
farewell.
        He stilled our longing.
135   He sang our sun-dried roots back into earth,
watered them: all-night rain of music so quiet
                                we could almost
        not hear it in the
                                moonless dark.
140 By dawn he was gone.
                        We have stood here since,
in our new life.
                We have waited.
                                He does not return.
145 It is said he made his earth-journey, and lost
        what he sought.
                It is said they felled him

---

1. knoll (nōl) *n.* small hill.

TAKE NOTES

and cut up his limbs for firewood.
                              And it is said
150 his head still sang and was swept out to sea singing.
Perhaps he will not return.
                              But what we have lived
comes back to us.
                    We see more.
155   We feel, as our rings increase,
something that lifts our branches, that stretches
      our furthest
                                        leaf-tips
further.
            The wind, the birds,
160   do not sound poorer but clearer,
recalling our agony, and the way we danced.
The music!

from An Enemy of the People

by Henrik Ibsen

TAKE NOTES

Background At the opening of the play, the future looks good for Dr. Thomas Stockmann's hometown. The town has finally opened a health resort for visitors, who come to drink and bathe in the local water, which is said to have healthful effects. Just when the town is beginning to benefit from the new business, however, Dr. Stockmann makes an alarming discovery. Sewage from a nearby industrial town is polluting the water. As Dr. Stockmann explains to his wife, his oldest child, Petra, and a few friends, the town will have to relocate the pipes that feed the baths in order to prevent the spread of disease. He has sent a report on the problem to his brother Peter, mayor of the town. The next morning, Peter pays him a visit.

MAYOR STOCKMANN. (*entering from the hall*). Good morning.

DR. STOCKMANN. Good to see you, Peter!

MRS. STOCKMANN. Morning, Peter. How's every thing with you?

MAYOR STOCKMANN. Just so-so, thank you. (*To the* DOCTOR.) Yesterday, after office hours, I received a report from you, discussing the condition of the water at the baths.

DR. STOCKMANN. Yes. Have you read it?

MAYOR STOCKMANN. I have.

DR. STOCKMANN. What have you got to say about it?

MAYOR STOCKMANN. (*glancing at the others*). Hm—

MRS. STOCKMANN. Come along, Petra.

(*She and* PETRA *go into the room on the left.*)

MAYOR STOCKMANN. (*after a moment*). Was it necessary to press all these investigations behind my back?

TAKE NOTES

____
____
____
____
____
____
____
____
____
____
____
____
____
____
____
____
____
____
____
____
____
____
____
____

Dr. Stockmann. Well, as long as I didn't have absolute proof, then—

Mayor Stockmann. And now you think you do?

Dr. Stockmann. You must be convinced of that yourself.

Mayor Stockmann. Is it your object to put this document before the board of directors by way of an official recommendation?

Dr. Stockmann. Of course. Something has to be done about this. And fast.

Mayor Stockmann. As usual, in your report you let your language get out of hand. You say, among other things, that what we're offering our summer visitors is guaranteed poison.

Dr. Stockmann. But, Peter, how else can you describe it? You've got to realize—this water is poison for internal or external use! And it's foisted on poor, suffering creatures who turn to us in good faith and pay us exorbitant fees to gain their health back again!

Mayor Stockmann. And then you arrive at the conclusion, by your line of reasoning, that we have to build a sewer to drain off these so-called impurities from Mølledal,[1] and that all the water mains have to be relaid.

Dr. Stockmann. Well, do you see any other way out? I don't.

Mayor Stockmann. I invented a little business this morning down at the town engineer's office. And in a half-joking way, I brought up these proposals as something we perhaps ought to take under advisement[2] at some time in the future.

Dr. Stockmann. Some time in the future!

Mayor Stockmann. He smiled at my whimsical extravagance—naturally. Have you gone to the trouble of estimating just what these proposed changes would cost? From the information I received, the expenditure would probably run up

---

1. **Mølledal** (möl′ ə däl′) fictional Norwegian town.
2. **to take under advisement** to think over carefully.

into several hundred thousand crowns.[3]

DR. STOCKMANN. As high as that?

MAYOR STOCKMANN. Yes. But that's not the worst. The work would extend over at least two years.

DR. STOCKMANN. Two years? Two full years?

MAYOR STOCKMANN. At the least. And meanwhile what do we do with the baths? Shut them down? Yes, we'll have to. Do you really think anyone would make the effort to come all the distance here if the rumor got out that the water was contaminated?

DR. STOCKMANN. Yes, but Peter, that's what it is.

MAYOR STOCKMANN. And then all this happens now— just now, when the baths were being recognized. Other towns in this area have the same resources for development as health resorts. Don't you think they'll leap at the chance to attract the whole flow of tourists to them? No question of it. And there we are, left stranded. We'll most likely have to abandon the whole costly enterprise; and then you'll have ruined the town you were born in.

DR. STOCKMANN. I—ruined—!

MAYOR STOCKMANN. It's through the baths alone that this town has any future to speak of. You can see that just as plain as I can.

DR. STOCKMANN. But then what do you think ought to be done?

MAYOR STOCKMANN. From your report I'm unable to persuade myself that the condition of the baths is as critical as you claim.

DR. STOCKMANN. Look, if anything, it's worse! Or it'll be that by summer, when the warm weather comes.

MAYOR STOCKMANN. Once again. I think you're exaggerating considerably. A capable doctor must know the right steps to take—he should be able to control toxic[4] elements, and to treat them if they make their presence too obvious.

DR. STOCKMANN. And then—? What else—?

---

3. **crowns** *n.* A crown is the Norwegian unit of currency; krone (krō´ nə).
4. **toxic** (täk´ sik) *adj.* poisonous.

TAKE NOTES

MAYOR STOCKMANN. The water system for the baths as it now stands is simply a fact and clearly has to be accepted as such. But in time the directors will more than likely agree to take under consideration to what extent—depending on the funds available—they can institute certain improvements.

DR. STOCKMANN. And you can think I'd play along with that kind of trickery!

MAYOR STOCKMANN. Trickery?

DR. STOCKMANN. Yes, it's a trick—a deception, a lie, an out-and-out crime against the public and society at large!

MAYOR STOCKMANN. As I've already observed, I've not yet persuaded myself that there's any real impending danger here.

DR. STOCKMANN. Yes, you have! There's no alternative. My report is perfectly accurate, I know that! And you're very much aware of it, Peter, but you won't admit it. You're the one who got the baths and the water system laid out where they are today; and it's this—it's this hellish miscalculation that you won't concede. Pah! You don't think I can see right through you?

MAYOR STOCKMANN. And even if it were true? Even if I seem a bit overanxious about my reputation, it's all for the good of the town. Without moral authority I could hardly guide and direct affairs in the way I believe serves the general welfare. For this reason—among many others—it strikes me as imperative[5] that your report not be submitted to the board of directors. It has to be withheld for the common good. Then, later, I'll bring the matter up for discussion, and we'll do the very best we can, as quietly as possible. But nothing—not the slightest word of this catastrophe must leak out to the public.

DR. STOCKMANN. My dear Peter, there's no stopping it now.

MAYOR STOCKMANN. It must and it will be stopped.

---

5. **imperative** (im per´ ə tiv) *adj.* absolutely necessary; urgent.

Dr. Stockmann. I'm telling you, it's no use. Too many people know already.

Mayor Stockmann. Know already! Who? Not those fellows from the *Courier*—?

Dr. Stockmann. Why, of course they know. The independent liberal press is going to see that you do your duty.

Mayor Stockmann (*after a short pause*). You're an exceptionally thoughtless man, Thomas. Haven't you considered the consequences that can follow for you?

Dr. Stockmann. Consequences? For me?

Mayor Stockmann. For you and your family as well.

Dr. Stockmann. What the devil does *that* mean?

Mayor Stockmann. I think, over the years, I've proved a helpful and accommodating brother to you.

Dr. Stockmann. Yes, you have, and I'm thankful to you for that.

Mayor Stockmann. I'm not after thanks. Because, in part, I was forced into it—for my own sake. I always hoped I could keep you in check somewhat if I helped better your economic status.

Dr. Stockmann. What? Just for your own sake—!

Mayor Stockmann. In part, I said. It's embarrassing for a public servant when his closest relative goes and compromises himself again and again.

Dr. Stockmann. And that's what you think I do?

Mayor Stockmann. Yes, unfortunately you do, without your knowing it. You have a restless, unruly, combative nature. And then this unhappy knack[6] of bursting into print on all kinds of likely and unlikely subjects. You're no sooner struck by an idea than right away you have to scribble a newspaper article on it, or a whole pamphlet even.

Dr. Stockmann. Well, but isn't it a citizen's duty to

---

6. **knack** (nak) *n.* trick; particular skill.

TAKE NOTES

____
____
____
____
____
____
____
____
____
____
____
____
____
____
____
____
____
____
____
____
____
____
____
____

inform the public if he comes on a new idea?

MAYOR STOCKMANN. Oh, the public doesn't need new ideas. The public is served best by the good, old, time-tested ideas it's always had.

DR. STOCKMANN. That's putting it plainly!

MAYOR STOCKMANN. I have to talk to you plainly for once. Up till now I've always tried to avoid that because I know how irritable you are; but now I'm telling you the truth, Thomas. You have no conception how much you injure yourself with your impetuosity. You complain about the authorities and, yes, the government; you rail against them—and insist you're being passed over and persecuted. But what can you expect—someone as troublesome as you.

DR. STOCKMANN. Ah—so I'm troublesome, too?

MAYOR STOCKMANN. Yes, Thomas, you're a very troublesome man to work with. I know from experience. You show no consideration at all. You seem to forget completely that I'm the one you can thank for your post here as staff physician at the baths—

DR. STOCKMANN. I was the inevitable[7] choice—I and nobody else! I was the first to see that this town could become a flourishing spa;[8] and I was the *only* one who could see it then. I stood alone fighting for that idea for years; and I wrote and wrote—

MAYOR STOCKMANN. Unquestionably. But the right moment hadn't arrived yet. Of course you couldn't judge that from up there in the wilds. But when the opportune time came, and I—and a few others—took the matter in hand—

DR. STOCKMANN. Yes, and bungled the whole magnificent plan. Oh yes, it's really coming out now what a brilliant crew you've been!

MAYOR STOCKMANN. All that's coming out, to my mind, is your usual hunger for a good fight. You want to attack your superiors—it's your old pattern. You can't stand any authority over you; you resent

---

7. inevitable (in ev´ i tə bəl) *adj.* certain to happen; that which cannot be avoided.
8. spa (spä) *n.* health resort where people drink and bathe in mineral waters.

anyone in a higher position and regard him as a
personal enemy—and then one weapon's as good
as another to use. But now I've acquainted you
with the vital interests at stake here for this whole
town—and, naturally, for me as well. And so I'm
warning you, Thomas, I'll be adamant about the
demand I am going to make of you.

Dr. Stockmann. What demand?

Mayor Stockmann. Since you've been so indiscreet as
to discuss this delicate issue with outsiders, even
though it should have been kept secret among the
directors, it of course can't be hushed up now.
All kinds of rumors will go flying around, and
the maliciously inclined will dress them up with
trimmings of their own. It'll therefore be necessary
that you publicly deny these rumors.

Dr. Stockmann. I! How? I don't understand.

Mayor Stockmann. We can expect that, after further
investigation, you'll arrive at the conclusion that
things are far from being as critical or dangerous as
you'd first imagined.

Dr. Stockmann. Ah—you expect that!

Mayor Stockmann. Moreover, we expect that you'll
support and publicly affirm your confidence
in the present directors to take thorough and
conscientious measures, as necessary, to remedy
any possible defects.

Dr. Stockmann. But that's utterly out of the question for
me, as long as they try to get by with patchwork.
I'm telling you that, Peter; and it's my unqualified
opinion—!

Mayor Stockmann. As a member of the staff, you're not
entitled to any personal opinions.

Dr. Stockmann. (*stunned*). Not entitled—?

Mayor Stockmann. As a staff member, I said. As a
private person—why, that's another matter. But
as a subordinate official at the baths, you're not
entitled to express any opinions that contradict
your superiors.

Dr. Stockmann. That's going too far! I, as a doctor, a

TAKE NOTES

man of science, aren't entitled to—!

Mayor Stockmann. What's involved here isn't a purely scientific problem. It's a mixture of both technical and economic considerations.

Dr. Stockmann. I don't care what the hell it is! I want the freedom to express myself on any problem under the sun!

Mayor Stockmann. Anything you like—except for the baths. We forbid you that.

Dr. Stockmann (*shouting*). You forbid—! You! A crowd of—!

Mayor Stockmann. *I* forbid it—*I*, your supervisor. And when I forbid you, then you obey.

The Tragedy of Julius Caesar, Act III

by William Shakespeare

Having ignored the warnings of the soothsayer in Act I and those of his wife, Calpurnia, in Act II, Caesar proceeds to the Capitol on the ides of March. Decius has told him that the Senate is ready to confer a crown upon him. Caesar is accompanied by the conspirators, led by Cassius and Brutus, as well as by his friend Mark Antony. Meanwhile, Artemidorus plans to reveal the conspiracy to Caesar. As Act III unfolds, Caesar approaches the Capitol, and events take a fateful, irreversible turn.

Act III

Scene i. Rome. Before the Capitol.

[*Flourish of trumpets. Enter* CAESAR, BRUTUS, CASSIUS, CASCA, DECIUS, METELLUS CIMBER, TREBONIUS, CINNA, ANTONY, LEPIDUS, ARTEMIDORUS, PUBLIUS, POPILIUS, *and the* SOOTHSAYER.]

CAESAR. The ides of March are come.

SOOTHSAYER. Ay, Caesar, but not gone.

ARTEMIDORUS. Hail, Caesar! Read this schedule.[1]

DECIUS. Trebonius doth desire you to o'er-read,
5   At your best leisure, this his humble suit.[2]

ARTEMIDORUS. O Caesar, read mine first; for mine's a suit
  That touches[3] Caesar nearer. Read it, great Caesar.

CAESAR. What touches us ourself shall be last served.

---

1. **schedule** (skej′ ool) *n.* paper.
2. **suit** *n.* petition; plea.
3. **touches** *v.* concerns.

TAKE NOTES

Artemidorus. Delay not, Caesar; read it instantly.

Caesar. What, is the fellow mad?

10 **Publius.**   Sirrah, give place.[4]

Cassius. What, urge you your petitions in the street?
Come to the Capitol.

[Caesar *goes to the Capitol, the rest following.*]

Popilius. I wish your enterprise today may thrive.

Cassius. What enterprise, Popilius?

Popilius.   Fare you well.

[*Advances to* Caesar]

15 **Brutus.** What said Popilius Lena?

Cassius. He wished today our enterprise might
thrive. I fear our purpose is discoverèd.

Brutus. Look how he makes to[5] Caesar; mark him.

Cassius. Casca, be sudden,[6] for we fear prevention.
20 Brutus, what shall be done? If this be known,
Cassius or Caesar never shall turn back,[7]
For I will slay myself.

Brutus.   Cassius, be constant.[8]
Popilius Lena speaks not of our purposes;
For look, he smiles, and Caesar doth not change.[9]

25 **Cassius.** Trebonius knows his time; for look you,
Brutus,
He draws Mark Antony out of the way.

[*Exit* Antony *and* Trebonius.]

Decius. Where is Metellus Cimber? Let him go
And presently prefer his suit[10] to Caesar.

Brutus. He is addressèd.[11] Press near and second[12]
him.

---

4. **give place** get out of the way.
5. **makes to** approaches.
6. **be sudden** be quick.
7. **Cassius . . . back** either Cassius or Caesar will not return alive.
8. **constant** *adj.* firm; calm.
9. **change** *v.* that is, change the expression on his face.
10. **presently prefer his suit** immediately present his petition.
11. **addressed** *adj.* ready.
12. **second** *v.* support.

30 **CINNA.** Casca, you are the first that rears your hand.

CAESAR. Are we all ready? What is now amiss
   That Caesar and his Senate must redress?[13]

METELLUS. Most high, most mighty, and most
      puissant[14] Caesar,
   Metellus Cimber throws before thy seat
   An humble heart.   [*Kneeling*]

35 **CAESAR.**   I must prevent thee, Cimber.
   These couchings and these lowly courtesies[15]
   Might fire the blood of ordinary men,
   And turn preordinance and first decree
   Into the law of children.[16] Be not fond[17]
40 To think that Caesar bears such rebel blood
   That will be thawed from the true quality[18]
   With that which melteth fools—I mean sweet
      words,
   Low-crookèd curtsies, and base spaniel fawning.[19]
   Thy brother by decree is banishèd.
45 If thou dost bend and pray and fawn for him,
   I spurn[20] thee like a cur out of my way.
   Know, Caesar doth not wrong, nor without cause
   Will he be satisfied.

METELLUS. Is there no voice more worthy than my
      own,
50 To sound more sweetly in great Caesar's ear
   For the repealing[21] of my banished brother?

BRUTUS. I kiss thy hand, but not in flattery, Caesar,
   Desiring thee that Publius Cimber may
   Have an immediate freedom of repeal.[22]

CAESAR. What, Brutus?

55 **CASSIUS.**   Pardon, Caesar; Caesar, pardon!
   As low as to thy foot doth Cassius fall
   To beg enfranchisement[23] for Publius Cimber.

---

13. **amiss . . . redress** wrong that Caesar and his Senate must correct.
14. **puissant** (pyo͞o´ i sənt) *adj.* powerful.
15. **couchings . . . courtesies** low bowings and humble gestures of reverence.
16. **And turn . . . law of children** and change what has already been decided as children might change their minds.
17. **fond** *adj.* foolish (enough).
18. **rebel . . . quality** unstable disposition that will lose its firmness.
19. **base spaniel fawning** low doglike cringing.
20. **spurn** *v.* kick disdainfully.
21. **repealing** *n.* recalling; ending the banishment.
22. **freedom of repeal** permission to be recalled.
23. **enfranchisement** (en fran´ chīz mənt) *n.* freedom.

The Tragedy of Julius Caesar, Act III **87**

TAKE NOTES

CAESAR. I could be well moved, if I were as you;
   If I could pray to move,[24] prayers would move me;
60   But I am constant as the Northern Star,
   Of whose true-fixed and resting[25] quality
   There is no fellow[26] in the firmament.[27]
   The skies are painted with unnumb'red sparks,
   They are all fire and every one doth shine;
65   But there's but one in all doth hold his[28] place.
   So in the world; 'tis furnished well with men,
   And men are flesh and blood, and apprehensive;[29]
   Yet in the number I do know but one
   That unassailable holds on his rank,[30]
70   Unshaked of motion;[31] and that I am he,
   Let me a little show it, even in this—
   That I was constant[32] Cimber should be banished,
   And constant do remain to keep him so.

CINNA. O Caesar—

CAESAR.   Hence! Wilt thou lift up Olympus?[33]

DECIUS. Great Caesar—

75 **CAESAR.**   Doth not Brutus bootless[34] kneel?

CASCA. Speak hands for me!   [*They stab* CAESAR.]

CAESAR. *Et tu, Brute?*[35] Then fall, Caesar.   [*Dies*]

CINNA. Liberty! Freedom! Tyranny is dead!
   Run hence, proclaim, cry it about the streets.

80 **CASSIUS.** Some to the common pulpits,[36] and cry out
   "Liberty, freedom, and enfranchisement!"

BRUTUS. People, and senators, be not affrighted.
   Fly not; stand still; ambition's debt is paid.[37]

---

24. pray to move beg others to change their minds.
25. resting *adj.* immovable.
26. fellow *n.* equal.
27. firmament (fur′mə mənt) *n.* sky.
28. his *pron.* its.
29. apprehensive (ap′ rə hen′ siv) *adj.* able to understand.
30. one/That unassailable . . . rank one who, unattackable, maintains his position.
31. Unshaked of motion unmoved by his own or others' impulses.
32. constant *adj.* determined.
33. Olympus (ō lim′ pəs) *n.* mountain in Greece on which the Greek gods were said to live.
34. bootless (boot′ lis) *adv.* uselessly.
35. Et tu, Brute? Latin for "And you, too, Brutus?"
36. pulpits (pul′ pits) *n.* speakers' platforms.
37. ambition's . . . paid ambition received what it deserved.

Casca. Go to the pulpit, Brutus.

Decius.   And Cassius too.

85 **Brutus.** Where's Publius?[38]

Cinna. Here, quite confounded with this mutiny.[39]

Metellus. Stand fast together, lest some friend of Caesar's
    Should chance—

Brutus. Talk not of standing. Publius, good cheer;
90   There is no harm intended to your person,
    Nor to no Roman else. So tell them, Publius.

Cassius. And leave us, Publius, lest that the people
    Rushing on us should do your age some mischief.

Brutus. Do so; and let no man abide[40] this deed
95   But we the doers.

[*Enter* Trebonius.]

Cassius. Where is Antony?

Trebonius.   Fled to his house amazed.[41]
    Men, wives, and children stare, cry out and run,
    As[42] it were doomsday.

Brutus.   Fates, we will know your pleasures.
    That we shall die, we know; 'tis but the time,
100   And drawing days out, that men stand upon.[43]

Casca. Why, he that cuts off twenty years of life
    Cuts off so many years of fearing death.

Brutus. Grant that, and then is death a benefit.
    So are we Caesar's friends, that have abridged
105   His time of fearing death. Stoop, Romans, stoop,
    And let us bathe our hands in Caesar's blood
    Up to the elbows, and besmear our swords.
    Then walk we forth, even to the market place,[44]
    And waving our red weapons o'er our heads,

---

38. **Publius** (pōōb′ lē əs) an elderly senator.
39. **mutiny** (myōōt′ 'n ē) *n.* revolt against authority, such as a rebellion of soldiers against their officers.
40. **let no man abide** let no man take responsibility for.
41. **amazed** *adj.* astounded.
42. **As** *conj.* as if.
43. **'tis but the time . . . upon** It is only the time of death and the length of life that people care about.
44. **market place** the open area of the Roman Forum, the center of government, business, and public life in ancient Rome.

The Tragedy of Julius Caesar, Act III **89**

TAKE NOTES

110   Let's all cry "Peace, freedom, and liberty!"

CASSIUS. Stoop then, and wash. How many ages hence
        Shall this our lofty scene be acted over
        In states unborn and accents yet unknown!

BRUTUS. How many times shall Caesar bleed in sport,[45]
115   That now on Pompey's basis lies along[46]
        No worthier than the dust!

CASSIUS.   So oft as that shall be,
        So often shall the knot[47] of us be called
        The men that gave their country liberty.

DECIUS. What, shall we forth?

CASSIUS.   Ay, every man away.
120   Brutus shall lead, and we will grace his heels[48]
        With the most boldest and best hearts of Rome.

[*Enter a* SERVANT.]

BRUTUS. Soft,[49] who comes here? A friend of Antony's.

SERVANT. Thus, Brutus, did my master bid me kneel;
        Thus did Mark Antony bid me fall down;
125   And, being prostrate, thus he bade me say:
        Brutus is noble, wise, valiant, and honest;
        Caesar was mighty, bold, royal,[50] and loving.
        Say I love Brutus and I honor him;
        Say I feared Caesar, honored him, and loved him.
130   If Brutus will vouchsafe that Antony
        May safely come to him and be resolved[51]
        How Caesar hath deserved to lie in death,
        Mark Antony shall not love Caesar dead
        So well as Brutus living; but will follow
135   The fortunes and affairs of noble Brutus
        Thorough the hazards of this untrod state[52]
        With all true faith. So says my master Antony.

---

45. **in sport** for amusement; the deed will be acted out in plays.
46. **on Pompey's basis lies along** by the pedestal of Pompey's statue lies stretched out.
47. **knot** *n.* group.
48. **grace his heels** do honor to his heels; follow him.
49. **Soft** *interjection* wait
50. **royal** *adj.* showing noble generosity.
51. **be resolved** have it explained.
52. **Thorough . . . state** through the dangers of this new state of affairs.

Brutus. Thy master is a wise and valiant Roman;
I never thought him worse.
140 Tell him, so[53] please him come unto this place,
He shall be satisfied and, by my honor,
Depart untouched.

Servant.   I'll fetch him presently.[54]

[*Exit* Servant]

Brutus. I know that we shall have him well to
friend.[55]

Cassius. I wish we may. But yet have I a mind
145 That fears him much; and my misgiving still
Falls shrewdly to the purpose.[56]

[*Enter* Antony.]

Brutus. But here comes Antony. Welcome, Mark
Antony.

Antony. O mighty Caesar! Dost thou lie so low?
Are all thy conquests, glories, triumphs, spoils,
150 Shrunk to this little measure? Fare thee well.
I know not, gentlemen, what you intend,
Who else must be let blood,[57] who else is rank.[58]
If I myself, there is no hour so fit
As Caesar's death's hour, nor no instrument
155 Of half that worth as those your swords, made
rich
With the most noble blood of all this world.
I do beseech ye, if you bear me hard,[59]
Now, whilst your purpled hands[60] do reek and
smoke,
Fulfill your pleasure. Live[61] a thousand years,
160 I shall not find myself so apt[62] to die;
No place will please me so, no mean of death,[63]
As here by Caesar, and by you cut off,
The choice and master spirits of this age.

---

53. so *conj.* if it should.
54. presently *adv.* immediately.
55. to friend as a friend.
56. my misgiving . . . to the purpose my doubts always turn out to be justified.
57. be let blood (a pun) "be bled for medical purposes" or "be killed."
58. rank (a pun) "too powerful" or "swollen with disease and therefore in need of bloodletting."
59. bear me hard have a grudge against me.
60. purpled hands bloody hands.
61. Live if I live.
62. apt *adj.* ready.
63. mean of death way of dying.

TAKE NOTES

BRUTUS. O Antony, beg not your death of us!
165   Though now we must appear bloody and cruel,
    As by our hands and this our present act
    You see we do, yet see you but our hands
    And this the bleeding business they have done.
    Our hearts you see not; they are pitiful;[64]
170   And pity to the general wrong of Rome—
    As fire drives out fire, so pity pity[65]—
    Hath done this deed on Caesar. For your part,
    To you our swords have leaden[66] points, Mark
       Antony:
    Our arms in strength of malice, and our hearts
175   Of brothers' temper,[67] do receive you in
    With all kind love, good thoughts, and reverence.

CASSIUS. Your voice[68] shall be as strong as any man's
    In the disposing of new dignities.[69]

BRUTUS. Only be patient till we have appeased
180   The multitude, beside themselves with fear,
    And then we will deliver[70] you the cause
    Why I, that did love Caesar when I struck him,
    Have thus proceeded.

ANTONY.   I doubt not of your wisdom.
    Let each man render me his bloody hand.
185   First, Marcus Brutus, will I shake with you;
    Next, Caius Cassius, do I take your hand;
    Now, Decius Brutus, yours; now yours, Metellus;
    Yours, Cinna; and, my valiant Casca, yours;
    Though last, not least in love, yours, good
       Trebonius.
190   Gentlemen all—alas, what shall I say?
    My credit[71] now stands on such slippery ground
    That one of two bad ways you must conceit[72] me,
    Either a coward or a flatterer.
    That I did love thee, Caesar, O, 'tis true!

---

64. pitiful *adj.* full of pity or compassion.
65. pity pity pity for Rome drove out pity for Caesar.
66. leaden *adj.* dull; blunt.
67. Our arms . . . / Of brothers' temper our arms strengthened with the desire to do harm and our hearts filled with brotherly feelings.
68. voice *n.* vote.
69. dignities *n.* offices.
70. deliver *v.* tell to.
71. credit *n.* reputation.
72. conceit (kən sēt´) *v.* think of.

195 If then thy spirit look upon us now,
Shall it not grieve thee dearer[73] than thy death
To see thy Antony making his peace,
Shaking the bloody fingers of thy foes,
Most noble, in the presence of thy corse?[74]
200 Had I as many eyes as thou hast wounds,
Weeping as fast as they stream forth thy blood,
It would become me better than to close[75]
In terms of friendship with thine enemies.
Pardon me, Julius! Here wast thou bayed,[76] brave
    hart;[77]
205 Here didst thou fall, and here thy hunters stand,
Signed in thy spoil[78] and crimsoned in thy
    Lethe.[79]
O world, thou wast the forest to this hart;
And this indeed, O world, the heart of thee.
How like a deer, stroken[80] by many princes.
210 Dost thou here lie!

CASSIUS. Mark Antony—

ANTONY.   Pardon me, Caius Cassius.
The enemies of Caesar shall say this;
Then, in a friend, it is cold modesty.[81]

CASSIUS. I blame you not for praising Caesar so;
215 But what compact[82] mean you to have with us?
Will you be pricked[83] in number of our friends,
Or shall we on,[84] and not depend on you?

ANTONY. Therefore I took your hands, but was indeed
Swayed from the point by looking down on
    Caesar.
220 Friends am I with you all, and love you all,
Upon this hope, that you shall give me reasons
Why, and wherein, Caesar was dangerous.

---

73. **dearer** *adv.* more deeply.
74. **corse** *n.* corpse.
75. **close** (clōz) *v.* reach an agreement.
76. **bayed** *v.* cornered.
77. **hart** (härt) *n.* deer.
78. **Signed in thy spoil** marked by signs of your slaughter.
79. **Lethe** (lē´ thē) river in Hades, the mythological Greek underworld inhabited by
    the dead; here, a river of blood.
80. **stroken** *v.* struck down.
81. **cold modesty** calm, moderate speech.
82. **compact** (käm´ pakt´) *n.* agreement.
83. **pricked** *v.* marked down; included.
84. **on** proceed.

TAKE NOTES

TAKE NOTES

____

____

____

____

____

____

____

____

____

____

____

____

____

____

____

____

____

____

____

____

____

____

____

____

BRUTUS. Or else were this a savage spectacle.
    Our reasons are so full of good regard[85]
225   That were you, Antony, the son of Caesar,
    You should be satisfied.

ANTONY.   That's all I seek;
    And am moreover suitor that I may
    Produce[86] his body to the market place,
    And in the pulpit, as becomes a friend,
230   Speak in the order[87] of his funeral.

BRUTUS. You shall, Mark Antony.

CASSIUS.   Brutus, a word with you.
    [*Aside to* BRUTUS] You know not what you do; do
       not consent
    That Antony speak in his funeral.
    Know you how much the people may be moved
    By that which he will utter?

235 **BRUTUS.**   By your pardon:
    I will myself into the pulpit first,
    And show the reason of our Caesar's death.
    What Antony shall speak, I will protest[88]
    He speaks by leave and by permission,
240   And that we are contented Caesar shall
    Have all true rites and lawful ceremonies.
    It shall advantage more than do us wrong.[89]

CASSIUS. I know not what may fall;[90] I like it not.

BRUTUS. Mark Antony, here, take you Caesar's body.
245   You shall not in your funeral speech blame us,
    But speak all good you can devise of Caesar,
    And say you do't by our permission;
    Else shall you not have any hand at all
    About his funeral. And you shall speak
250   In the same pulpit whereto I am going,
    After my speech is ended.

ANTONY.   Be it so;
    I do desire no more.

---

85. **so full of good regard** so carefully considered.
86. **Produce** *v.* bring forth.
87. **order** *n.* course of the ceremonies.
88. **protest** *v.* declare.
89. **advantage . . . wrong** benefit us more than hurt us.
90. **what may fall** what may happen.

Brutus. Prepare the body then, and follow us.

[*Exit all but* Antony.]

Antony. O pardon me, thou bleeding piece of earth,
255   That I am meek and gentle with these butchers!
  Thou art the ruins of the noblest man
  That ever livèd in the tide of times.[91]
  Woe to the hand that shed this costly blood!
  Over thy wounds now do I prophesy
260   (Which like dumb mouths do ope their ruby lips
  To beg the voice and utterance of my tongue),
  A curse shall light upon the limbs of men;
  Domestic fury and fierce civil strife
  Shall cumber[92] all the parts of Italy;
265   Blood and destruction shall be so in use,[93]
  And dreadful objects so familiar,
  That mothers shall but smile when they behold
  Their infants quartered with the hands of war,
  All pity choked with custom of fell deeds;[94]
270   And Caesar's spirit, ranging[95] for revenge,
  With Ate[96] by his side come hot from hell,
  Shall in these confines[97] with a monarch's voice
  Cry "Havoc,"[98] and let slip[99] the dogs of war,
  That this foul deed shall smell above the earth
275   With carrion[100] men, groaning for burial.

[*Enter* Octavius' Servant.]

  You serve Octavius Caesar, do you not?

Servant. I do, Mark Antony.

Antony. Caesar did write for him to come to Rome.

Servant. He did receive his letters and is coming,
280   And bid me say to you by word of mouth—
  O Caesar!   [*Seeing the body*]

---

  91. tide of times course of all history.
  92. cumber (kum´ bər) *v.* distress; burden.
  93. in use customary.
  94. custom of fell deeds being used to cruel acts.
  95. ranging *adj.* roaming like a wild beast in search of prey.
  96. Ate (ā´ tē) Greek goddess personifying criminal folly or reckless ambition in people.
  97. confines (kän´ fīnz) *n.* boundaries.
  98. Havoc Latin for "no quarter," a signal for general slaughter.
  99. let slip release from a leash.
  100. carrion (kar´ ē ən) *adj.* dead and rotting.

TAKE NOTES

ANTONY. Thy heart is big;[101] get thee apart and weep.
    Passion, I see, is catching, for mine eyes,
    Seeing those beads of sorrow stand in thine,
285   Began to water. Is thy master coming?

SERVANT. He lies tonight within seven leagues[102] of
    Rome.

ANTONY. Post[103] back with speed, and tell him what
    hath chanced.[104]
    Here is a mourning Rome, a dangerous Rome,
    No Rome of safety for Octavius yet.
290   Hie hence and tell him so. Yet stay awhile;
    Thou shalt not back till I have borne this corse
    Into the market place; there shall I try[105]
    In my oration[106] how the people take
    The cruel issue[107] of these bloody men;
295   According to the which, thou shalt discourse
    To young Octavius of the state of things.
    Lend me your hand.   [*Exit*]

Scene ii. The Forum

[*Enter* BRUTUS *and goes into the pulpit, and* CASSIUS, *with the* PLEBEIANS.[1]]

PLEBEIANS. We will be satisfied![2] Let us be satisfied!

BRUTUS. Then follow me, and give me audience,
    friends.
    Cassius, go you into the other street
    And part the numbers.[3]
5   Those that will hear me speak, let 'em stay here;
    Those that will follow Cassius, go with him;
    And public reasons shall be renderèd
    Of Caesar's death.

FIRST PLEBEIAN.   I will hear Brutus speak.

---

101. **big** *adj.* swollen with grief.
102. **leagues** (lēgz) *n.* units of measure, each equivalent in Roman times to about a mile and a half.
103. **Post** *v.* hasten.
104. **hath chanced** has happened.
105. **try** *v.* test.
106. **oration** (ō rā´ shən) *n.* formal public speech.
107. **cruel issue** outcome of the cruelty.

---

1. **Plebeians** (pli bē´ ənz) *n.* commoners; members of the lower class.
2. **be satisfied** get an explanation.
3. **part the numbers** divide the crowd.

Second Plebeian. I will hear Cassius, and compare their reasons,

10 When severally[4] we hear them renderèd.

[*Exit* Cassius, *with some of the* Plebeians.]

Third Plebeian. The noble Brutus is ascended. Silence!

Brutus. Be patient till the last.
Romans, countrymen, and lovers,[5] hear me for my cause, and be silent, that you may hear. Believe me
15 for mine honor, and have respect to mine honor, that
you may believe. Censure[6] me in your wisdom, and awake your senses,[7] that you may the better judge. If
there be any in this assembly, any dear friend of Caesar's, to him I say that Brutus' love to Caesar was
20 no less than his. If then that friend demand why Brutus rose against Caesar, this is my answer: Not that I loved Caesar less, but that I loved Rome more. Had you rather Caesar were living, and die all slaves,
than that Caesar were dead, to live all free men? As
25 Caesar loved me, I weep for him; as he was fortunate,
I rejoice at it; as he was valiant, I honor him; but, as he was ambitious, I slew him. There is tears, for his love; joy, for his fortune; honor, for his valor; and death, for his ambition. Who is here so base,[8] that
30 would be a bondman?[9] If any, speak; for him have I offended. Who is here so rude,[10] that would not be a Roman? If any, speak; for him have I offended. Who is
here so vile,[11] that will not love his country? If any, speak; for him have I offended. I pause for a reply.

35 **All.** None, Brutus, none!

---

4. **severally** (sev´ ər əl ē) *adv.* separately.
5. **lovers** *n.* dear friends.
6. **Censure** (sen´ shər) *v.* judge.
7. **senses** *n.* powers of reason.
8. **base** *adj.* low.
9. **bondman** *n.* slave.
10. **rude** *adj.* uncivilized.
11. **vile** (vīl) *adj.* mean; low-born; of low character.

TAKE NOTES

TAKE NOTES

Brutus. Then none have I offended. I have done no
more to Caesar than you shall do to Brutus. The
question of his death is enrolled in the Capitol;[12]
his
glory not extenuated,[13] wherein he was worthy, nor
40   his offenses enforced,[14] for which he suffered death.

[*Enter* Mark Antony, *with* Caesar's *body.*]

Here comes his body, mourned by Mark Antony,
who, though he had no hand in his death, shall
receive
the benefit of his dying, a place in the
commonwealth,
as which of you shall not? With this I depart, that,
as
45   I slew my best lover for the good of Rome, I have the
same dagger for myself, when it shall please my
country to need my death.

All. Live, Brutus! Live, live!

First Plebeian. Bring him with triumph home unto
his house.

50   **Second Plebeian.** Give him a statue with his
ancestors.

Third Plebeian. Let him be Caesar.

Fourth Plebeian.   Caesar's better parts[15]
Shall be crowned in Brutus.

First Plebeian. We'll bring him to his house with
shouts and clamors.

Brutus. My countrymen—

Second Plebeian.   Peace! Silence! Brutus speaks.

55   **First Plebeian.** Peace, ho!

Brutus. Good countrymen, let me depart alone,
And, for my sake, stay here with Antony.
Do grace to Caesar's corpse, and grace his speech
Tending to Caesar's glories,[16] which Mark Antony

---

12. **The question . . . in the Capitol** The issues that led to his death are on record
in the Capitol.
13. **extenuated** (ek sten′ yo͞o āt′ id) *adj.* undervalued; made less of.
14. **enforced** (en fôrst′) *adj.* exaggerated.
15. **parts** *n.* qualities.
16. **Do grace . . . glories** Show respect for Caesar's body and for the speech
telling of Caesar's achievements.

60   By our permission, is allowed to make.
I do entreat you, not a man depart,
Save I alone, till Antony have spoke.   [*Exit*]

FIRST PLEBEIAN. Stay, ho! And let us hear Mark
     Antony.

THIRD PLEBEIAN. Let him go up into the public chair;
65   We'll hear him. Noble Antony, go up.

ANTONY. For Brutus' sake, I am beholding[17] to you.

FOURTH PLEBEIAN. What does he say of Brutus?

THIRD PLEBEIAN.   He says, for Brutus' sake,
He finds himself beholding to us all.

FOURTH PLEBEIAN. 'Twere best he speak no harm of
     Brutus here!

FIRST PLEBEIAN. This Caesar was a tyrant.

70   **THIRD PLEBEIAN.**   Nay, that's certain.
We are blest that Rome is rid of him.

SECOND PLEBEIAN. Peace! Let us hear what Antony can
     say.

ANTONY. You gentle Romans—

ALL.   Peace, ho! Let us hear him.

ANTONY. Friends, Romans, countrymen, lend me
     your ears;
75   I come to bury Caesar, not to praise him.
The evil that men do lives after them,
The good is oft interrèd with their bones;
So let it be with Caesar. The noble Brutus
Hath told you Caesar was ambitious.
80   If it were so, it was a grievous fault,
And grievously hath Caesar answered[18] it.
Here, under leave of Brutus and the rest
(For Brutus is an honorable man,
So are they all, all honorable men),
85   Come I to speak in Caesar's funeral.
He was my friend, faithful and just to me;
But Brutus says he was ambitious,
And Brutus is an honorable man.
He hath brought many captives home to Rome,

---

17. beholding *adj.* indebted.
18. answered *v.* paid the penalty for.

TAKE NOTES

90 Whose ransoms did the general coffers[19] fill;
Did this in Caesar seem ambitious?
When that the poor have cried, Caesar hath wept;
Ambition should be made of sterner stuff.
Yet Brutus says he was ambitious;
95 And Brutus is an honorable man.
You all did see that on the Lupercal
I thrice presented him a kingly crown,
Which he did thrice refuse. Was this ambition?
Yet Brutus says he was ambitious;
100 And sure he is an honorable man.
I speak not to disprove what Brutus spoke,
But here I am to speak what I do know.
You all did love him once, not without cause;
What cause withholds you then to mourn for
    him?
105 O judgment, thou art fled to brutish beasts,
And men have lost their reason! Bear with me;
My heart is in the coffin there with Caesar,
And I must pause till it come back to me.

First Plebeian. Methinks there is much reason in his
    sayings.

110 **Second Plebeian.** If thou consider rightly of the matter,
    Caesar has had great wrong.

Third Plebeian.   Has he, masters?
I fear there will a worse come in his place.

Fourth Plebeian. Marked ye his words? He would not
    take the crown,
Therefore 'tis certain he was not ambitious.

115 **First Plebeian.** If it be found so, some will dear abide
    it.[20]

Second Plebeian. Poor soul, his eyes are red as fire
    with weeping.

Third Plebeian. There's not a nobler man in Rome than
    Antony.

Fourth Plebeian. Now mark him, he begins again to
    speak.

Antony. But yesterday the word of Caesar might

---

19. **general coffers** public treasury.
20. **dear abide it** pay dearly for it.

120 Have stood against the world; now lies he there,
And none so poor to[21] do him reverence.
O masters! If I were disposed to stir
Your hearts and minds to mutiny and rage,
I should do Brutus wrong and Cassius wrong,
125 Who, you all know, are honorable men.
I will not do them wrong; I rather choose
To wrong the dead, to wrong myself and you,
Than I will wrong such honorable men.
But here's a parchment with the seal of Caesar;
130 I found it in his closet; 'tis his will.
Let but the commons[22] hear this testament,
Which, pardon me, I do not mean to read,
And they would go and kiss dead Caesar's
     wounds,
And dip their napkins[23] in his sacred blood;
135 Yea, beg a hair of him for memory,
And dying, mention it within their wills,
Bequeathing it as a rich legacy
Unto their issue.[24]

FOURTH PLEBEIAN. We'll hear the will; read it, Mark
     Antony.

140 **ALL.** The will, the will! We will hear Caesar's will!

ANTONY. Have patience, gentle friends, I must not
     read it.
It is not meet[25] you know how Caesar loved you.
You are not wood, you are not stones, but men;
And being men, hearing the will of Caesar,
145 It will inflame you, it will make you mad.
'Tis good you know not that you are his heirs;
For if you should, O, what would come of it?

FOURTH PLEBEIAN. Read the will! We'll hear it, Antony!
You shall read us the will, Caesar's will!

150 **ANTONY.** Will you be patient? Will you stay awhile?
I have o'ershot myself[26] to tell you of it.
I fear I wrong the honorable men
Whose daggers have stabbed Caesar; I do fear it.

FOURTH PLEBEIAN. They were traitors. Honorable men!

---

21. **so poor to** low enough in rank to.
22. **commons** *n.* plebeians; commoners.
23. **napkins** *n.* handkerchiefs.
24. **issue** *n.* children; offspring.
25. **meet** *adj.* fitting; suitable.
26. **o'ershot myself** gone further than I meant to.

The Tragedy of Julius Caesar, Act III **101**

TAKE NOTES

155   **ALL**. The will! The testament!

  SECOND PLEBEIAN. They were villains, murderers! The will!
Read the will!

  ANTONY. You will compel me then to read the will?
Then make a ring about the corpse of Caesar,
160   And let me show you him that made the will.
Shall I descend? And will you give me leave?

  ALL. Come down.

  SECOND PLEBEIAN. Descend.   [ANTONY *comes down*.]

  THIRD PLEBEIAN. You shall have leave.

165   **FOURTH PLEBEIAN**. A ring! Stand round.

  FIRST PLEBEIAN. Stand from the hearse,[27] stand from the body!

  SECOND PLEBEIAN. Room for Antony, most noble Antony!

  ANTONY. Nay, press not so upon me; stand far[28] off.

  ALL. Stand back! Room! Bear back.

170   **ANTONY**. If you have tears, prepare to shed them now.
You all do know this mantle;[29] I remember
The first time ever Caesar put it on:
'Twas on a summer's evening, in his tent,
That day he overcame the Nervii.[30]
175   Look, in this place ran Cassius' dagger through;
See what a rent[31] the envious[32] Casca made;
Through this the well-belovèd Brutus stabbed,
And as he plucked his cursèd steel away,
Mark how the blood of Caesar followed it,
180   As[33] rushing out of doors, to be resolved[34]
If Brutus so unkindly[35] knocked, or no;
For Brutus, as you know, was Caesar's angel.
Judge, O you gods, how dearly Caesar loved him!
This was the most unkindest cut of all;

---

27. **hearse** (hʉrs) *n.* coffin.
28. **far** *adv.* farther.
29. **mantle** (man´ təl) *n.* cloak; toga.
30. **Nervii** (nʉr´ vē ī) *n.* warlike European tribe conquered by Caesar in 57 B.C.
31. **rent** *n.* hole; tear; rip.
32. **envious** (en´ vē əs) *adj.* spiteful.
33. **As** *conj.* as if.
34. **to be resolved** to learn for certain.
35. **unkindly** *adj.* cruelly; also, unnaturally.

185 For when the noble Caesar saw him stab,
Ingratitude, more strong than traitors' arms,
Quite vanquished him. Then burst his mighty
     heart;
And, in his mantle muffling up his face,
Even at the base of Pompey's statue
190 (Which all the while ran blood) great Caesar fell.
O, what a fall was there, my countrymen!
Then I, and you, and all of us fell down,
Whilst bloody treason flourished[36] over us.
O, now you weep, and I perceive you feel
195 The dint[37] of pity; these are gracious drops.
Kind souls, what[38] weep you when you but behold
Our Caesar's vesture[39] wounded? Look you here,
Here is himself, marred as you see with[40] traitors.

FIRST PLEBEIAN. O piteous spectacle!

200 **SECOND PLEBEIAN.** O noble Caesar!

THIRD PLEBEIAN. O woeful day!

FOURTH PLEBEIAN. O traitors, villains!

FIRST PLEBEIAN. O most bloody sight!

SECOND PLEBEIAN. We will be revenged.

205 **ALL.** Revenge! About![41] Seek! Burn! Fire! Kill! Slay!
     Let not a traitor live!

ANTONY. Stay, countrymen.

FIRST PLEBEIAN. Peace there! Hear the noble Antony.

SECOND PLEBEIAN. We'll hear him, we'll follow him,
     we'll die
210 with him!

ANTONY. Good friends, sweet friends, let me not stir
     you up
To such a sudden flood of mutiny.
They that have done this deed are honorable.
What private griefs[42] they have, alas, I know not,

---

36. flourished (flur′ isht) *v.* swaggered; waved a sword in triumph.
37. dint *n.* stroke; blow.
38. what *adv.* why.
39. vesture (ves′ chər) *n.* clothing.
40. with *prep.* by.
41. About let's go.
42. private griefs personal grievances.

TAKE NOTES

215 That made them do it. They are wise and
honorable,
And will, no doubt, with reasons answer you.
I come not, friends, to steal away your hearts;
I am no orator, as Brutus is;
But (as you know me all) a plain blunt man
220 That love my friend, and that they know full well
That gave me public leave to speak[43] of him.
For I have neither writ, nor words, nor worth,
Action, or utterance,[44] nor the power of speech
To stir men's blood; I only speak right on.[45]
225 I tell you that which you yourselves do know,
Show you sweet Caesar's wounds, poor poor
dumb mouths,
And bid them speak for me. But were I Brutus,
And Brutus Antony, there were an Antony
Would ruffle up your spirits, and put a tongue
230 In every wound of Caesar's that should move
The stones of Rome to rise and mutiny.

ALL. We'll mutiny.

FIRST PLEBEIAN. We'll burn the house of Brutus.

THIRD PLEBEIAN. Away, then! Come, seek the
conspirators.

ANTONY. Yet hear me, countrymen. Yet hear me speak.

235 **ALL.** Peace, ho! Hear Antony, most noble Antony!

ANTONY. Why, friends, you go to do you know not what:
Wherein
hath Caesar thus deserved your loves?
Alas, you know not; I must tell you then: You
have forgot the
will I told you of.

240 **ALL.** Most true, the will! Let's stay and hear the will.

ANTONY. Here is the will, and under Caesar's seal.
To every Roman citizen he gives,
To every several[46] man, seventy-five drachmas.

SECOND PLEBEIAN. Most noble Caesar! We'll revenge
his death!

---

43. **public leave to speak** permission to speak in public.
44. **neither writ . . . utterance** (ut′ ər əns) neither a written speech, nor fluency,
nor reputation, nor gestures, nor style of speaking.
45. **right on** directly.
46. **several** *adj.* individual.

245 **THIRD PLEBEIAN.** O royal[47] Caesar!

ANTONY. Hear me with patience.

ALL. Peace, ho!

ANTONY. Moreover, he hath left you all his walks,
His private arbors, and new-planted orchards,[48]
250 On this side Tiber; he hath left them you,
And to your heirs forever: common pleasures,[49]
To walk abroad and recreate yourselves.
Here was a Caesar! When comes such another?

FIRST PLEBEIAN. Never, never! Come, away, away!
255 We'll burn his body in the holy place,
And with the brands[50] fire the traitors' houses.
Take up the body.

SECOND PLEBEIAN. Go fetch fire.

THIRD PLEBEIAN. Pluck down benches.

260 **FOURTH PLEBEIAN.** Pluck down forms, windows,[51]
anything!

[*Exit* PLEBEIANS *with the body.*]

ANTONY. Now let it work:[52] Mischief, thou art afoot,
Take thou what course thou wilt.

[*Enter* SERVANT.]
How now, fellow?

SERVANT. Sir, Octavius is already come to Rome.

ANTONY. Where is he?

265 **SERVANT.** He and Lepidus are at Caesar's house.

ANTONY. And thither[53] will I straight to visit him;
He comes upon a wish.[54] Fortune is merry,
And in this mood will give us anything.

SERVANT. I heard him say, Brutus and Cassius
270 Are rid[55] like madmen through the gates of Rome.

---

47. royal *adj.* showing noble generosity.
48. walks . . . orchards parks, his private stands of trees, and newly planted gardens.
49. common pleasures public places of recreation.
50. brands *n.* torches.
51. forms, windows benches and shutters.
52. work *v.* spread and expand, as yeast does; follow through to a conclusion.
53. thither *adv.* there.
54. upon a wish as I wished.
55. Are rid have ridden.

TAKE NOTES

ANTONY. Belike[56] they had some notice of the people,[57]
How I had moved them. Bring me to Octavius.

[*Exit*]

Scene iii. A street.

[*Enter* CINNA THE POET, *and after him the* PLEBEIANS.]

CINNA. I dreamt tonight[1] that I did feast with Caesar,
And things unluckily charge my fantasy.[2]
I have no will to wander forth of doors,[3]
Yet something leads me forth.

5   **FIRST PLEBEIAN.** What is your name?

SECOND PLEBEIAN. Whither are you going?

THIRD PLEBEIAN. Where do you dwell?

FOURTH PLEBEIAN. Are you a married man or a bachelor?

SECOND PLEBEIAN. Answer every man directly.[4]

10   **FIRST PLEBEIAN.** Ay, and briefly.

FOURTH PLEBEIAN. Ay, and wisely.

THIRD PLEBEIAN. Ay, and truly, you were best.

CINNA. What is my name? Whither am I going? Where do I
dwell? Am I a married man or a bachelor? Then, to answer
15   every man directly and briefly, wisely and truly: wisely I say,
I am a bachelor.

SECOND PLEBEIAN. That's as much as to say, they are fools that
marry; you'll bear me a bang[5] for that, I fear. Proceed directly.

20   **CINNA.** Directly, I am going to Caesar's funeral.

FIRST PLEBEIAN. As a friend or an enemy?

---

56. Belike *adv.* probably.
57. notice of the people word about the mood of the people.

1. tonight *adv.* last night.
2. things . . . fantasy the events that have happened give an unlucky meaning to my dream.
3. forth of doors outdoors.
4. directly *adv.* in a straightforward manner.
5. bear me a bang get a blow from me.

Cinna. As a friend.

Second Plebeian. That matter is answered directly.

Fourth Plebeian. For your dwelling, briefly.

25 **Cinna.** Briefly, I dwell by the Capitol.

Third Plebeian. Your name, sir, truly.

Cinna. Truly, my name is Cinna.

First Plebeian. Tear him to pieces! He's a
conspirator.

Cinna. I am Cinna the poet! I am Cinna the poet!

30 **Fourth Plebeian.** Tear him for his bad verses! Tear
him
for his bad verses!

Cinna. I am not Cinna the conspirator.

Fourth Plebeian. It is no matter, his name's Cinna;
pluck but
his name out of his heart, and turn him going.[6]

35 **Third Plebeian.** Tear him, tear him! [*They attack
him.*]
Come, brands, ho! Firebrands![7] To Brutus', to
Cassius'!
Burn all! Some to Decius' house, and some to
Casca's; some to Ligarius'! Away, go!

[*Exit all the* Plebeians *with* Cinna.]

---

6. **turn him going** send him on his way.
7. **Firebrands** *n.* burning pieces of wood; also, people who stir up others to
revolt.

Antigone

by Sophocles

translated by Dudley Fitts and Robert Fitzgerald

Persons Represented

ANTIGONE (an tig´ ə nē´), daughter of Oedipus, former King of Thebes

ISMENE (is mē´ nē), another daughter of Oedipus

EURYDICE (yōō rid´ i sē´), wife of Creon

CREON (krē´ än´), King of Thebes, uncle of Antigone and Ismene

HAIMON (hī´ mən), Creon's son, engaged to Antigone

TEIRESIAS (tī rē´ sē əs), a blind prophet

A SENTRY

A MESSENGER

CHORUS

CHORAGOS (kō rā´v gəs), leader of the chorus

A BOY who leads Teiresias

GUARDS

SERVANTS

Prologue–Scene 2

Scene. *Before the palace of* CREON, *King of Thebes. A central double door, and two lateral doors. A platform extends the length of the facade, and from this platform three steps lead down into the "orchestra," or chorus-ground.*

Time. *Dawn of the day after the repulse of the Argive[1] army from the assault on Thebes.*

PROLOGUE

[ANTIGONE *and* ISMENE *enter from the central door of the Palace.*]

    ANTIGONE. Ismene, dear sister,
        You would think that we had already suffered enough
        For the curse on Oedipus:[2]
        I cannot imagine any grief

---

1. **Argive** (är´ gīv´) from Argos, the capital of a section of ancient Greece.
2. **curse on Oedipus** reference to the fate of Oedipus, who was doomed by a decree of the gods to kill his father and marry his mother while ignorant of their true identities.

5   That you and I have not gone through. And now—
       Have they told you of the new decree of our King
          Creon?

   ISMENE. I have heard nothing: I know
       That two sisters lost two brothers, a double death
       In a single hour; and I know that the Argive army
10   Fled in the night; but beyond this, nothing.

   ANTIGONE. I thought so. And that is why I wanted you
       To come out here with me. There is something we
          must do.

   ISMENE. Why do you speak so strangely?

   ANTIGONE. Listen, Ismene:
15   Creon buried our brother Eteocles
       With military honors, gave him a soldier's funeral,
       And it was right that he should; but Polyneices,
       Who fought as bravely and died as miserably,—
       They say that Creon has sworn
20   No one shall bury him, no one mourn for him,
       But his body must lie in the fields, a sweet treasure
       For carrion birds[3] to find as they search for food.
       That is what they say, and our good Creon is
          coming here
       To announce it publicly; and the penalty—
25   Stoning to death in the public square!
                                        There it is,
       And now you can prove what you are:
       A true sister, or a traitor to your family.

   ISMENE. Antigone, you are mad! What could I
          possibly do?

30 **ANTIGONE.** You must decide whether you will help me
          or not.

   ISMENE. I do not understand you. Help you in what?

   ANTIGONE. Ismene, I am going to bury him. Will you
          come?

   ISMENE. Bury him! You have just said the new law
          forbids it.

---

3. carrion (kar′ ē ən) **birds** scavenger birds, such as vultures.

TAKE NOTES

ANTIGONE. He is my brother. And he is your brother, too.

35 **ISMENE.** But think of the danger! Think what Creon will do!

ANTIGONE. Creon is not strong enough to stand in my way.

ISMENE. Ah sister!
Oedipus died, everyone hating him
For what his own search brought to light, his eyes
40 Ripped out by his own hand; and Iocaste died,
His mother and wife at once: she twisted the cords
That strangled her life; and our two brothers died,
Each killed by the other's sword. And we are left:
But oh, Antigone,
45 Think how much more terrible than these
Our own death would be if we should go against Creon
And do what he has forbidden! We are only women,
We cannot fight with men, Antigone!
The law is strong, we must give in to the law
50 In this thing, and in worse. I beg the Dead
To forgive me, but I am helpless: I must yield
To those in authority. And I think it is dangerous business
To be always meddling.

ANTIGONE. If that is what you think,
55 I should not want you, even if you asked to come.
You have made your choice, you can be what you want to be.
But I will bury him; and if I must die,
I say that this crime is holy: I shall lie down
With him in death, and I shall be as dear
60 To him as he to me.
It is the dead,
Not the living, who make the longest demands;
We die for ever . . .
You may do as you like,
65 Since apparently the laws of the gods mean nothing to you.

Ismene. They mean a great deal to me; but I
    have no strength
To break laws that were made for the public good.

Antigone. That must be your excuse, I
    suppose. But as for me,
I will bury the brother I love.

70 **Ismene.**   Antigone,
I am so afraid for you!

Antigone.   You need not be:
You have yourself to consider, after all.

Ismene. But no one must hear of this,
    you must tell no one!
75 I will keep it a secret, I promise!

Antigone.   Oh tell it! Tell everyone!
Think how they'll hate you when it all comes out
If they learn that you knew about it all the time!

Ismene. So fiery! You should be cold with fear.

80 **Antigone.** Perhaps. But I am doing only what I must.

Ismene. But can you do it? I say that you cannot.

Antigone. Very well: when my strength gives out, I
    shall do no more.

Ismene. Impossible things should not be tried at all.

Antigone. Go away, Ismene:
85 I shall be hating you soon, and the dead will too,
For your words are hateful. Leave me my foolish
    plan:
I am not afraid of the danger; if it means death,
It will not be the worst of deaths—death without
    honor.

Ismene. Go then, if you feel that you must.
90 You are unwise,
But a loyal friend indeed to those who love you.

[*Exit into the Palace.* Antigone *goes off, left. Enter the*
Chorus.]

TAKE NOTES

PARODOS

CHORUS.   [STROPHE 1]
Now the long blade of the sun, lying
Level east to west, touches with glory
Thebes of the Seven Gates.[4] Open, unlidded
Eye of golden day! O marching light
5   Across the eddy and rush of Dirce's stream,[5]
Striking the white shields of the enemy
Thrown headlong backward from the blaze
    of morning!

CHORAGOS. Polyneices their commander
Roused them with windy phrases,
10   He the wild eagle screaming
Insults above our land,
His wings their shields of snow,
His crest their marshalled helms.

CHORUS.   [ANTISTROPHE 1]
Against our seven gates in a yawning ring
15   The famished spears came onward in the night;
But before his jaws were sated with our blood,
Or pinefire took the garland of our towers,
He was thrown back; and as he turned, great
    Thebes—
No tender victim for his noisy power—
20   Rose like a dragon behind him, shouting war.

CHORAGOS. For God hates utterly
The bray of bragging tongues;
And when he beheld their smiling,
Their swagger of golden helms,
25   The frown of his thunder blasted
Their first man from our walls.

CHORUS.   [STROPHE 2]
We heard his shout of triumph high in the air
Turn to a scream; far out in a flaming arc
He fell with his windy torch, and the earth struck
    him.
30   And others storming in fury no less than his
Found shock of death in the dusty joy of battle.

---

4. **Seven Gates** The city of Thebes was defended by walls containing seven
entrances.
5. **Dirce's** (dʉr′ sēz) **stream** small river near Thebes into which the body of Dirce,
one of the city's early queens, was thrown after her murder.

Choragos. Seven captains at seven gates
    Yielded their clanging arms to the god
    That bends the battle-line and breaks it.
35   These two only, brothers in blood,
    Face to face in matchless rage,
    Mirroring each the other's death,
    Clashed in long combat.

Chorus.   [Antistrophe 2]
    But now in the beautiful morning of victory
40   Let Thebes of the many chariots sing for joy!
    With hearts for dancing we'll take leave of war:
    Our temples shall be sweet with hymns of praise,
    And the long night shall echo with our chorus.

Scene 1

Choragos. But now at last our new King is coming:
    Creon of Thebes, Menoikeus'[6] son.
    In this auspicious dawn of his reign
    What are the new complexities
5   That shifting Fate has woven for him?
    What is his counsel? Why has he summoned
    The old men to hear him?

[*Enter* Creon *from the Palace, center. He addresses the* Chorus *from the top step.*]

Creon. Gentlemen: I have the honor to inform you that our
    Ship of State, which recent storms have threatened to
10   destroy, has come safely to harbor at last, guided by the
    merciful wisdom of Heaven. I have summoned you here this
    morning because I know that I can depend upon you: your
    devotion to King Laïos was absolute; you never hesitated in
    your duty to our late ruler Oedipus; and when Oedipus died,
15   your loyalty was transferred to his children. Unfortunately,

---

6. Menoikeus' (me noiʹ kē us əz)

Antigone **113**

TAKE NOTES

____

____

____

____

____

____

____

____

____

____

____

____

____

____

____

____

____

____

____

____

____

____

____

as you know, his two sons, the princes Eteocles and
Polyneices, have killed each other in battle; and I, as
the next in blood, have suceeded to the full power
of the throne.

20 I am aware, of course, that no Ruler can expect
      complete
loyalty from his subjects until he has been tested in
office. Nevertheless, I say to you at the very outset
that I have nothing but con tempt for the kind of
Governor who is afraid, for whatever reason, to follow

25 the course that he knows is best for the State;
      and as for
the man who sets private friendship above the
      public
welfare,—I have no use for him, either. I call God to
witness that if I saw my country headed for ruin, I
should not be afraid to speak out plainly; and I need

30 hardly remind you that I would never have any
      dealings
with an enemy of the people. No one values
      friendship more
highly than I; but we must remember that friends
      made at
the risk of wrecking our Ship are not real friends
      at all.
These are my principles, at any rate, and that is
      why I

35 have made the following decision concerning the
      sons of
Oedipus: Eteocles, who died as a man should die,
fighting for his country, is to be buried with full
      military
honors, with all the ceremony that is usual when
      the greatest
heroes die; but his brother Polyneices, who broke
      his

40 exile to come back with fire and sword against his
      native
city and the shrines of his fathers' gods, whose
      one idea
was to spill the blood of his blood and sell his
      own people into
slavery—Polyneices, I say, is to have no burial: no
      man is to
touch him or say the least prayer for him; he
      shall lie

45   on the plain, unburied; and the birds and the
        scavenging
    dogs can do with him whatever they like.
  This is my command, and you can see the wisdom
      behind
    it. As long as I am King, no traitor is going to be
      honored
    with the loyal man. But whoever shows by word
      and
50   deed that he is on the side of the State,—he
      shall have
    my respect while he is living, and my reverence
      when he
    is dead.

CHORAGOS. If that is your will, Creon son of Menoikeus,
    You have the right to enforce it: we are yours.

55   **CREON.** That is my will. Take care that you do your
    part.

CHORAGOS. We are old men: let the younger ones
    carry it out.

CREON. I do not mean that: the sentries have been
    appointed.

CHORAGOS. Then what is it that you would have us
    do?

CREON. You will give no support to whoever breaks
    this law.

60   **CHORAGOS.** Only a crazy man is in love with death!

CREON. And death it is; yet money talks, and the
    wisest
    Have sometimes been known to count a few coins
    too many.

[*Enter* SENTRY *from left.*]

SENTRY. I'll not say that I'm out of breath from
    running, King,
    because every time I stopped to think about what
    I have to
65   tell you, I felt like going back. And all the time a
    voice kept
    saying, "You fool, don't you know you're walking
    straight into

trouble?"; and then another voice: "Yes, but if you let somebody else get the news to Creon first, it will be even worse
than that for you!" But good sense won out, at least I hope
70 it was good sense, and here I am with a story that makes
no sense at all; but I'll tell it anyhow, because, as they say,
what's going to happen's going to happen, and—

CREON. Come to the point. What have you to say?

SENTRY. I did not do it. I did not see who did it. You must not
75 punish me for what someone else has done.

CREON. A comprehensive defense! More effective, perhaps,
If I knew its purpose. Come: what is it?

SENTRY. A dreadful thing . . . I don't know how to put it—

CREON. Out with it!

80 **SENTRY.**   Well, then;
The dead man—
              Polyneices—

[*Pause. The* SENTRY *is overcome, fumbles for words.*
CREON *waits impassively.*]
                              out there—

                              someone,—

85 New dust on the slimy flesh!

[*Pause. No sign from* CREON.]

Someone has given it burial that way, and
Gone . . .

[*Long pause.* CREON *finally speaks with deadly control.*]

CREON. And the man who dared do this?

SENTRY.   I swear I
90 Do not know! You must believe me!

                              Listen:
The ground was dry, not a sign of digging, no,

Not a wheeltrack in the dust, no trace of anyone.
It was when they relieved us this morning: and
    one of them,

95 The corporal, pointed to it.
                            There it was,
The strangest—
                Look:
The body, just mounded over with light dust: you
    see?
100 Not buried really, but as if they'd covered it
Just enough for the ghost's peace. And no sign
Of dogs or any wild animal that had been there.

And then what a scene there was! Every man of us
Accusing the other: we all proved the other man
    did it,
105 We all had proof that we could not have done it.
We were ready to take hot iron in our hands,
Walk through fire, swear by all the gods,
It was not I!
I do not know who it was, but it was not I!

[CREON's *rage has been mounting steadily, but the* SENTRY
is too intent upon his story to notice it.]

110 And then, when this came to nothing, someone
    said
A thing that silenced us and made us stare
Down at the ground: you had to be told the news,
And one of us had to do it! We threw the dice,
And the bad luck fell to me. So here I am,
115 No happier to be here than you are to have me:
Nobody likes the man who brings bad news.

CHORAGOS. I have been wondering, King: can it be
    that the
gods have done this?

CREON. [*Furiously*] Stop!
Must you doddering wrecks
120 Go out of your heads entirely? "The gods!"
Intolerable!
The gods favor this corpse? Why? How had he
    served them?
Tried to loot their temples, burn their images,
Yes, and the whole State, and its laws with it!

TAKE NOTES

125 Is it your senile opinion that the gods love to
    honor bad men?
A pious thought!—
    No, from the very beginning
There have been those who have whispered
    together,
Stiff-necked anarchists, putting their heads
    together,
130 Scheming against me in alleys. These are the men,
And they have bribed my own guard to do this
    thing.
Money!   [*Sententiously*]
There's nothing in the world so demoralizing as
    money.
Down go your cities,
135 Homes gone, men gone, honest hearts corrupted,
Crookedness of all kinds, and all for money!
[*To* SENTRY]   But you—!
I swear by God and by the throne of God,
The man who has done this thing shall pay for it!
140 Find that man, bring him here to me, or your death
Will be the least of your problems: I'll string you
    up
Alive, and there will be certain ways to make you
Discover your employer before you die;
And the process may teach you a lesson you seem
    to have missed:
145 The dearest profit is sometimes all too dear:
That depends on the source. Do you understand
    me?
A fortune won is often misfortune.

SENTRY. King, may I speak?

CREON.   Your very voice distresses me.

150 **SENTRY.** Are you sure that it is my voice, and not
    your conscience?

CREON. By God, he wants to analyze me now!

SENTRY. It is not what I say, but what has been done,
    that hurts you.

CREON. You talk too much.

SENTRY.   Maybe; but I've done nothing.

155 **CREON.** Sold your soul for some silver: that's all
    you've done.

SENTRY. How dreadful it is when the right judge
   judges wrong!

CREON. Your figures of speech
   May entertain you now; but unless you bring me
      the man,
   You will get little profit from them in the end.

[*Exit* CREON *into the Palace.*]

160 **SENTRY.** "Bring me the man"—!
   I'd like nothing better than bringing him the man!
   But bring him or not, you have seen the last of
      me here.
   At any rate, I am safe!

[*Exit* SENTRY.]

ODE I

CHORUS.   [STROPHE 1]
   Numberless are the world's wonders, but none
   More wonderful than man; the stormgray sea
   Yields to his prows, the huge crests bear him
      high;
   Earth, holy and inexhaustible, is graven
5 With shining furrows where his plows have gone
   Year after year, the timeless labor of stallions.
                                              [ANTISTROPHE 1]
   The lightboned birds and beasts that cling to
      cover,
   The lithe fish lighting their reaches of dim water,
   All are taken, tamed in the net of his mind;
10 The lion on the hill, the wild horse windy-maned,
   Resign to him; and his blunt yoke has broken
   The sultry shoulders of the mountain bull.
                                              [STROPHE 2]
   Words also, and thought as rapid as air,
   He fashions to his good use; statecraft is his,
15 And his the skill that deflects the arrows of snow,
   The spears of winter rain: from every wind
   He has made himself secure—from all but one:
   In the late wind of death he cannot stand.
                                              [ANTISTROPHE 2]
   O clear intelligence, force beyond all measure!

Antigone **119**

TAKE NOTES

20 O fate of man, working both good and evil!
When the laws are kept, how proudly his city
    stands!
When the laws are broken, what of his city then?
Never may the anarchic man find rest at my
    hearth,
Never be it said that my thoughts are his
    thoughts.

SCENE 2

[*Re-enter* SENTRY *leading* ANTIGONE.]

    CHORAGOS. What does this mean? Surely this captive
        woman
    Is the Princess, Antigone. Why should she be
        taken?

    SENTRY. Here is the one who did it! We caught her
    In the very act of burying him.—Where is Creon?

5   **CHORAGOS.** Just coming from the house.

[*Enter* CREON, *center.*]

    CREON.   What has happened?
    Why have you come back so soon?

    SENTRY. [*Expansively*]   O King,
    A man should never be too sure of anything:
10   I would have sworn
    That you'd not see me here again: your anger
    Frightened me so, and the things you
        threatened me with;
    But how could I tell then
    That I'd be able to solve the case so soon?

15   No dice-throwing this time: I was only too
        glad to come!
    Here is this woman. She is the guilty one:
    We found her trying to bury him.
    Take her, then; question her; judge her as you
        will.
    I am through with the whole thing now, and glad
        of it.

20   **CREON.** But this is Antigone! Why have you brought
    her here?

    SENTRY. She was burying him, I tell you!

CREON. [*Severely*]   Is this the truth?

SENTRY. I saw her with my own eyes. Can I say
more?

CREON. The details: come, tell me quickly!

25 **SENTRY.**   It was like this:
After those terrible threats of yours, King,
We went back and brushed the dust away from
the body.
The flesh was soft by now, and stinking,
So we sat on a hill to windward and kept guard.
30 No napping this time! We kept each other awake.
But nothing happened until the white round sun
Whirled in the center of the round sky over us:
Then, suddenly,
A storm of dust roared up from the earth, and the
sky
35 Went out, the plain vanished with all its trees
In the stinging dark. We closed our eyes and
endured it.
The whirlwind lasted a long time, but it passed;
And then we looked, and there was Antigone!
I have seen
40 A mother bird come back to a stripped nest,
heard
Her crying bitterly a broken note or two
For the young ones stolen. Just so, when this girl
Found the bare corpse, and all her love's work
wasted,
She wept, and cried on heaven to damn the
hands
45 That had done this thing.
                    And then she brought more dust
And sprinkled wine three times for her brother's
ghost.
We ran and took her at once. She was not afraid,
Not even when we charged her with what she had
done.
50 She denied nothing.
                    And this was a comfort to me,
And some uneasiness: for it is a good thing
To escape from death, but it is no great pleasure
To bring death to a friend.

TAKE NOTES

55   Yet I always say
There is nothing so comfortable as your own safe
    skin!

CREON. [*Slowly, dangerously*] And you, Antigone,

    You with your head hanging,—do you confess this
    thing?

ANTIGONE. I do. I deny nothing.

60   **CREON.** [*To* SENTRY]   You may go.
                                  [*Exit* SENTRY.]

    [*To* ANTIGONE] Tell me, tell me briefly:
    Had you heard my proclamation touching this
    matter?

ANTIGONE. It was public. Could I help hearing it?

CREON. And yet you dared defy the law.

65   **ANTIGONE.**   I dared.
    It was not God's proclamation. That final Justice
    That rules the world below makes no such laws.
    Your edict, King, was strong,
    But all your strength is weakness itself against
70   The immortal unrecorded laws of God.
    They are not merely now: they were, and shall be,
    Operative forever, beyond man utterly.
    I knew I must die, even without your decree:
    I am only mortal. And if I must die
75   Now, before it is my time to die,
    Surely this is no hardship: can anyone
    Living, as I live, with evil all about me,
    Think Death less than a friend? This death of
      mine
    Is of no importance; but if I had left my brother
80   Lying in death unburied, I should have suffered.
    Now I do not.
            You smile at me. Ah Creon,
    Think me a fool, if you like; but it may well be
    That a fool convicts me of folly.

85   **CHORAGOS.** Like father, like daughter: both head
      strong, deaf to reason!
    She has never learned to yield.

CREON.   She has much to learn.
The inflexible heart breaks first, the toughest iron
Cracks first, and the wildest horses bend their
    necks
90 At the pull of the smallest curb.
                              Pride? In a slave?
This girl is guilty of a double insolence,
Breaking the given laws and boasting of it.
Who is the man here,
95 She or I, if this crime goes unpunished?
Sister's child, or more than sister's child,
Or closer yet in blood—she and her sister
Win bitter death for this!
[*To* SERVANTS]   Go, some of you,
100 Arrest Ismene. I accuse her equally.
Bring her: you will find her sniffling in the house
    there.
Her mind's a traitor: crimes kept in the dark
Cry for light, and the guardian brain shudders;
But how much worse than this
105 Is brazen boasting of barefaced anarchy!

ANTIGONE. Creon, what more do you want than my
    death?

CREON.   Nothing.
That gives me everything.

ANTIGONE.   Then I beg you: kill me.
110 This talking is a great weariness: your words
Are distasteful to me, and I am sure that mine
Seem so to you. And yet they should not seem so:
I should have praise and honor for what I have
    done.
All these men here would praise me
115 Were their lips not frozen shut with fear of you.
                              [*Bitterly*]
Ah the good fortune of kings,
Licensed to say and do whatever they please!

CREON. You are alone here in that opinion.

ANTIGONE. No, they are with me. But they keep their
    tongues in leash.

120 **CREON.** Maybe. But you are guilty, and they are not.

TAKE NOTES

ANTIGONE. There is no guilt in reverence for the dead.

CREON. But Eteocles—was he not your brother too?

ANTIGONE. My brother too.

CREON. And you insult his memory?

125 **ANTIGONE.** [*Softly*] The dead man would not say that I
insult it.

CREON. He would: for you honor a traitor as much as
him.

ANTIGONE. His own brother, traitor or not, and equal
in blood.

CREON. He made war on his country. Eteocles
defended it.

ANTIGONE. Nevertheless, there are honors due all the
dead.

130 **CREON.** But not the same for the wicked as for the
just.

ANTIGONE. Ah Creon, Creon,
Which of us can say what the gods hold wicked?

CREON. An enemy is an enemy, even dead.

ANTIGONE. It is my nature to join in love, not hate.

135 **CREON.** [*Finally losing patience*] Go join them, then; if
you must have your love,
Find it in hell!

CHORAGOS. But see, Ismene comes:

[*Enter* ISMENE, *guarded.*]

Those tears are sisterly, the cloud
That shadows her eyes rains down gentle sorrow.

140 **CREON.** You too, Ismene,
Snake in my ordered house, sucking my blood
Stealthily—and all the time I never knew
That these two sisters were aiming at my throne!
Ismene,

145 Do you confess your share in this crime, or deny
it?
Answer me.

ISMENE. Yes, if she will let me say so. I am guilty.

ANTIGONE. [*Coldly*] No, Ismene. You have no right to
    say so.
    You would not help me, and I will not have you
    help me.

150 **ISMENE.** But now I know what you meant; and I am
    here
    To join you, to take my share of punishment.

ANTIGONE. The dead man and the gods who rule the
    dead
    Know whose act this was. Words are not friends.

ISMENE. Do you refuse me, Antigone? I want to die
    with you:

155   I too have a duty that I must discharge to the
    dead.

ANTIGONE. You shall not lessen my death by sharing
    it.

ISMENE. What do I care for life when you are dead?

ANTIGONE. Ask Creon. You're always hanging on his
    opinions.

ISMENE. You are laughing at me. Why, Antigone?

160 **ANTIGONE.** It's a joyless laughter, Ismene.

ISMENE.   But can I do nothing?

ANTIGONE. Yes. Save yourself. I shall not envy you.
    There are those who will praise you; I shall have
    honor, too.

ISMENE. But we are equally guilty!

165 **ANTIGONE.**   No more, Ismene.
    You are alive, but I belong to Death.

CREON. [*To the* CHORUS] Gentlemen, I beg you to
    observe these girls:
    One has just now lost her mind; the other,
    It seems, has never had a mind at all.

170 **ISMENE.** Grief teaches the steadiest minds to waver,
    King.

CREON. Yours certainly did, when you assumed guilt
    with the guilty!

ISMENE. But how could I go on living without her?

TAKE NOTES

CREON. You are.
She is already dead.

175 **ISMENE.** But your own son's bride!

CREON. There are places enough for him to push his
plow.
I want no wicked women for my sons!

ISMENE. O dearest Haimon, how your father wrongs
you!

CREON. I've had enough of your childish talk of
marriage!

180 **CHORAGOS.** Do you really intend to steal this girl from
your son?

CREON. No; Death will do that for me.

CHORAGOS. Then she must die?

CREON. [*Ironically*] You dazzle me.
—But enough of this talk!

185 [*To* GUARDS] You, there, take them away and guard
them well:
For they are but women, and even brave men run
When they see Death coming.

[*Exit* ISMENE, ANTIGONE, *and* GUARDS.]

ODE II

CHORUS. [STROPHE 1]

Fortunate is the man who has never tasted God's
vengeance!
Where once the anger of heaven has struck, that
house is shaken
For ever: damnation rises behind each child
Like a wave cresting out of the black northeast,

5 When the long darkness under sea roars up
And bursts drumming death upon the wind
whipped sand.

[ANTISTROPHE 1]

I have seen this gathering sorrow from time long
past
Loom upon Oedipus' children: generation from
generation
Takes the compulsive rage of the enemy god.

10   So lately this last flower of Oedipus' line
      Drank the sunlight! but now a passionate word
      And a handful of dust have closed up all its
          beauty.

                                    [Strophe 2]

      What mortal arrogance
      Transcends the wrath of Zeus?[7]
15   Sleep cannot lull him, nor the effortless long
          months
      Of the timeless gods: but he is young for ever,
      And his house is the shining day of high
          Olympos.[8]
            All that is and shall be,
            And all the past, is his.
20   No pride on earth is free of the curse of heaven.
                              [Antistrophe 2]

      The straying dreams of men
        May bring them ghosts of joy:
      But as they drowse, the waking embers burn
          them;
      Or they walk with fixed eyes, as blind men walk.
25   But the ancient wisdom speaks for our own time:
        Fate works most for woe
        With Folly's fairest show.
      Man's little pleasure is the spring of sorrow.

---

7. Zeus (zo͞os) King of all Greek gods, he was believed to throw lightning bolts
when angry.

8. Olympos (ō lim′ pəs) mountain in Greece where the gods were believed to live
in ease and splendor (also spelled "Olympus").

TAKE NOTES

TAKE NOTES

SCENE 3

CHORAGOS. But here is Haimon, King, the last of all
    your sons.
Is it grief for Antigone that brings him here,
And bitterness at being robbed of his bride?

[*Enter* HAIMON.]

CREON. We shall soon see, and no need of diviners.[1]
5   —Son,
You have heard my final judgment on that girl:
Have you come here hating me, or have you come
With deference and with love, whatever I do?

HAIMON. I am your son, father. You are my guide.
10 You make things clear for me, and I obey you.
No marriage means more to me than your
    continuing wisdom.

CREON. Good. That is the way to behave: subordinate
Everything else, my son, to your father's will.
This is what a man prays for, that he may get
15 Sons attentive and dutiful in his house,
Each one hating his father's enemies,
Honoring his father's friends. But if his sons
Fail him, if they turn out unprofitably,
What has he fathered but trouble for himself
20 And amusement for the malicious?
                            So you are right
Not to lose your head over this woman.
Your pleasure with her would soon grow cold,
    Haimon,
And then you'd have a hellcat in bed and else
    where.
25 Let her find her husband in Hell!
Of all the people in this city, only she
Has had contempt for my law and broken it.
Do you want me to show myself weak before the
    people?
Or to break my sworn word? No, and I will not.
30 The woman dies.
I suppose she'll plead "family ties." Well, let her.
If I permit my own family to rebel,

---

1. **diviners** (də vīn′ ərz) *n.* those who claim to forecast the future.

How shall I earn the world's obedience?
Show me the man who keeps his house in hand,
He's fit for public authority.
                              I'll have no dealings
With law-breakers, critics of the government:
Whoever is chosen to govern should be obeyed—
Must be obeyed, in all things, great and small,
Just and unjust! O Haimon,
The man who knows how to obey, and that man
    only,
Knows how to give commands when the time
    comes.
You can depend on him, no matter how fast
The spears come: he's a good soldier, he'll stick it
    out.

Anarchy, anarchy! Show me a greater evil!
This is why cities tumble and the great houses
    rain down,
This is what scatters armies!

No, no: good lives are made so by discipline.
We keep the laws then, and the lawmakers,

And no woman shall seduce us. If we must lose,
Let's lose to a man, at least! Is a woman stronger
    than we?

Choragos. Unless time has rusted my wits,
What you say, King, is said with point and
    dignity.

Haimon. [*Boyishly earnest*] Father:
Reason is God's crowning gift to man, and you
    are right
To warn me against losing mine. I cannot say—
I hope that I shall never want to say!—that you
Have reasoned badly. Yet there are other men
Who can reason, too; and their opinions might be
    helpful.
You are not in a position to know everything
That people say or do, or what they feel:
Your temper terrifies them—everyone
Will tell you only what you like to hear.
But I, at any rate, can listen; and I have heard
    them

TAKE NOTES

65 Muttering and whispering in the dark about this
  girl.
They say no woman has ever, so unreasonably,
Died so shameful a death for a generous act:
"She covered her brother's body. Is this indecent?
She kept him from dogs and vultures. Is this a
  crime?
70 Death?—She should have all the honor that we
  can give her!"

This is the way they talk out there in the city.

You must believe me:
Nothing is closer to me than your happiness.
What could be closer? Must not any son
75 Value his father's fortune as his father does his?
I beg you, do not be unchangeable:
Do not believe that you alone can be right.
The man who thinks that,
The man who maintains that only he has the
  power
80 To reason correctly, the gift to speak, the soul—
A man like that, when you know him, turns out
  empty.

It is not reason never to yield to reason!

In flood time you can see how some trees bend,
And because they bend, even their twigs are safe,
85 While stubborn trees are torn up, roots and all.
And the same thing happens in sailing:
Make your sheet fast, never slacken,—and over
  you go,
Head over heels and under: and there's your voy
  age.
Forget you are angry! Let yourself be moved!
90 I know I am young; but please let me say this:
The ideal condition
Would be, I admit, that men should be right by
  instinct;
But since we are all too likely to go astray,
The reasonable thing is to learn from those who
  can teach.

95 **CHORAGOS.** You will do well to listen to him, King,
  If what he says is sensible. And you, Haimon,
  Must listen to your father.—Both speak well.

CREON. You consider it right for a man of my years and experience
To go to school to a boy?

100 **HAIMON.**   It is not right
If I am wrong. But if I am young, and right,
What does my age matter?

CREON. You think it right to stand up for an anarchist?

HAIMON. Not at all. I pay no respect to criminals.

105 **CREON.** Then she is not a criminal?

HAIMON. The City would deny it, to a man.

CREON. And the City proposes to teach me how to rule?

HAIMON. Ah. Who is it that's talking like a boy now?

CREON. My voice is the one voice giving orders in this City!

110 **HAIMON.** It is no City if it takes orders from one voice.

CREON. The State is the King!

HAIMON.   Yes, if the State is a desert.

[*Pause*]

CREON. This boy, it seems, has sold out to a woman.

HAIMON. If you are a woman: my concern is only for you.

115 **CREON.** So? Your "concern"! In a public brawl with your father!

HAIMON. How about you, in a public brawl with justice?

CREON. With justice, when all that I do is within my rights?

HAIMON. You have no right to trample on God's right.

CREON. [*Completely out of control*] Fool, adolescent fool! Taken in by a woman!

TAKE NOTES

120   **HAIMON.** You'll never see me taken in by anything vile.

CREON. Every word you say is for her!

HAIMON. [*Quietly, darkly*]   And for you.
And for me. And for the gods under the earth.

CREON. You'll never marry her while she lives.

125   **HAIMON.** Then she must die.—But her death will
cause another.

CREON. Another?
Have you lost your senses? Is this an open
threat?

HAIMON. There is no threat in speaking to emptiness.

CREON. I swear you'll regret this superior tone of
yours!
130   You are the empty one!

HAIMON.   If you were not my father,
I'd say you were perverse.

CREON. You girlstruck fool, don't play at words with
me!

HAIMON. I am sorry. You prefer silence.

135   **CREON.**   Now, by God—!
I swear, by all the gods in heaven above us,
You'll watch it, I swear you shall!
[*To the* SERVANTS]   Bring her out!
Bring the woman out! Let her die before his eyes!
140   Here, this instant, with her bridegroom beside her!

HAIMON. Not here, no; she will not die here, King.
And you will never see my face again.
Go on raving as long as you've a friend to endure
you.

                         [*Exit* HAIMON.]

CHORAGOS. Gone, gone.
145   Creon, a young man in a rage is dangerous!

CREON. Let him do, or dream to do, more than a
man can.
He shall not save these girls from death.

CHORAGOS.   These girls?
You have sentenced them both?

150 **Creon.**   No, you are right.
   I will not kill the one whose hands are clean.

Choragos. But Antigone?

   Creon. [*Somberly*]   I will carry her far away
   Out there in the wilderness, and lock her
155 Living in a vault of stone. She shall have food,
   As the custom is, to absolve the State of her
      death.
   And there let her pray to the gods of hell:
   They are her only gods:
   Perhaps they will show her an escape from death,
160 Or she may learn,
                    though late,
   That piety shown the dead is pity in vain.

                                        [*Exit* Creon.]

Ode III

   Chorus. Love, unconquerable   [Strophe 1]
   Waster of rich men, keeper
   Of warm lights and all-night vigil
   In the soft face of a girl:
5 Sea-wanderer, forest-visitor!
   Even the pure Immortals cannot escape you,
   And mortal man, in his one day's dusk,
   Trembles before your glory.
   Surely you swerve upon ruin   [Antistrophe]
10 The just man's consenting heart,
   As here you have made bright anger
   Strike between father and son—
   And none has conquered but Love!
   A girl's glance working the will of heaven:

15 Pleasure to her alone who mocks us,
   Merciless Aphrodite.[2]

---

2. Aphrodite (af′ rə dīt′ ē) goddess of beauty and love who is sometimes vengeful
in her retaliation for offenses.

TAKE NOTES

SCENE 4

CHORAGOS. [*As* ANTIGONE *enters guarded*] But I can no
    longer stand in awe of this,
  Nor, seeing what I see, keep back my tears.
  Here is Antigone, passing to that chamber
  Where all find sleep at last.

5 **ANTIGONE.** Look upon me, friends, and pity me

                            [STROPHE 1]

  Turning back at the night's edge to say
  Good-by to the sun that shines for me no longer;
  Now sleepy Death
  Summons me down to Acheron,[3] that cold shore:

10 There is no bridesong there, nor any music.

  CHORUS. Yet not unpraised, not without a kind of
    honor,
  You walk at last into the underworld;
  Untouched by sickness, broken by no sword.
  What woman has ever found your way to death?

  ANTIGONE   [ANTISTROPHE 1]

15 How often I have heard the story of Niobe,[4]
  Tantalos'[5] wretched daughter, how the stone
  Clung fast about her, ivy-close: and they say
  The rain falls endlessly
  And sifting soft snow; her tears are never done.

20 I feel the loneliness of her death in mine.

  CHORUS. But she was born of heaven, and you
  Are woman, woman-born. If her death is yours,
  A mortal woman's, is this not for you
  Glory in our world and in the world beyond?

  ANTIGONE.   [STROPHE 2]

25 You laugh at me. Ah, friends, friends,
  Can you not wait until I am dead? O Thebes,
  O men many-charioted, in love with Fortune,

---

3. **Acheron** (ak´ ər än´) In Greek mythology, river in the underworld over which the dead are ferried.

4. **Niobe** (nī´ ō bē´) a queen of Thebes who was turned to stone while weeping for her slain children. Her seven sons and seven daughters were killed by Artemis and Apollo, the divine twins of Leto, after Leto complained that Niobe insulted her by bragging of maternal superiority. It was Zeus who turned the bereaved Niobe to stone, but her lament continued and her tears created a stream.

5. **Tantalos'** (tan´ tə lus əz) Niobe's father, who was condemned to eternal frustration in the underworld because he revealed the secrets of the gods.

Dear springs of Dirce, sacred Theban grove,
Be witnesses for me, denied all pity,
30 Unjustly judged! and think a word of love
For her whose path turns
Under dark earth, where there are no more tears.

Chorus. You have passed beyond human daring and come at last
Into a place of stone where Justice sits.
35 I cannot tell
What shape of your father's guilt appears in this.

Antigone.   [Antistrophe 2]
You have touched it at last: that bridal bed
Unspeakable, horror of son and mother mingling:
Their crime, infection of all our family!
40 O Oedipus, father and brother!
Your marriage strikes from the grave to murder mine.
I have been a stranger here in my own land:
All my life
The blasphemy of my birth has followed me.

45 **Chorus.** Reverence is a virtue, but strength
Lives in established law: that must prevail.
You have made your choice,
Your death is the doing of your conscious hand.

Antigone.   [Epode]
Then let me go, since all your words are bitter,
50 And the very light of the sun is cold to me.
Lead me to my vigil, where I must have
Neither love nor lamentation: no song, but silence.

[Creon *interrupts impatiently*.]

Creon. If dirges and planned lamentations could put off death,
Men would be singing forever.
55 [*To the* servants]   Take her, go!
You know your orders: take her to the vault
And leave her alone there. And if she lives or dies,
That's her affair, not ours: our hands are clean.

ANTIGONE. O tomb, vaulted bride-bed in eternal rock,

60   Soon I shall be with my own again
Where Persephone[6] welcomes the thin ghosts
    underground:
And I shall see my father again, and you, mother,
And dearest Polyneices—
                      dearest indeed

65   To me, since it was my hand
That washed him clean and poured the ritual wine:
And my reward is death before my time!

And yet, as men's hearts know, I have done no
    wrong,
I have not sinned before God. Or if I have,

70   I shall know the truth in death. But if the guilt
Lies upon Creon who judged me, then, I pray,
May his punishment equal my own.

CHORAGOS.   O passionate heart,
    Unyielding, tormented still by the same winds!

75 **CREON.** Her guards shall have good cause to regret
    their delaying.

ANTIGONE. Ah! That voice is like the voice of death!

CREON. I can give you no reason to think you are
    mistaken.

ANTIGONE. Thebes, and you my fathers' gods,
And rulers of Thebes, you see me now, the last

80   Unhappy daughter of a line of kings,
Your kings, led away to death. You will remember
What things I suffer, and at what men's hands,
Because I would not transgress the laws of
    heaven.

                      [*To the* GUARDS, *simply*]

Come: let us wait no longer

                      [*Exit* ANTIGONE, *left, guarded.*]

---

6. **Persephone** (pər sef′ ə nē) queen of the underworld.

ODE IV

CHORUS.   [STROPHE 1]

All Danae's beauty[7] was locked away
In a brazen cell where the sunlight could not
    come:
A small room, still as any grave, enclosed her.
Yet she was a princess too,
5   And Zeus in a rain of gold poured love upon her.
O child, child,
No power in wealth or war
Or tough sea-blackened ships
Can prevail against untiring Destiny!

                    [ANTISTROPHE 1]

10 And Dryas' son[8] also, that furious king,
Bore the god's prisoning anger for his pride:
Sealed up by Dionysos[9] in deaf stone,
His madness died among echoes.
So at the last he learned what dreadful power

15 His tongue had mocked:
For he had profaned the revels,
And fired the wrath of the nine
Implacable Sisters[10] that love the sound of the
    flute.

                    [STROPHE 2]

And old men tell a half-remembered tale
20 Of horror done where a dark ledge splits the sea
And a double surf beats on the gray shores:
How a king's new woman, sick
With hatred for the queen he had imprisoned,
Ripped out his two sons' eyes with her bloody
    hands

---

7. Danae's (dan′ ā ēz′) **beauty** Danae was imprisoned when it was foretold that she would mother a son who would kill her father, King Acrisios. Her beauty attracted Zeus, who visited her in the form of a shower of gold. Perseus was born of the union, and Danae was exiled with the child. Years later, as prophesied, the boy did kill Acrisios, whom he failed to recognize as his grandfather.

8. Dryas' (drī′ us əz) **son** Lycorgos (lī kɥr′ gəs), whose opposition to the worship of Dionysos was severely punished by the gods. He drove the followers of Dionysos from Thrace and was driven insane. Lycorgos recovered from his madness while imprisoned in a cave, but he was later blinded by Zeus as additional punishment.

9. Dionysos (dī ə nī′ səs) god of wine, in whose honor the Greek plays were performed.

10. nine / Implacable Sisters nine Muses, or goddesses, of science and literature. Implacable (im plak′ ə bəl) means "unforgiving."

TAKE NOTES

25 While grinning Ares[11] watched the shuttle plunge
Four times: four blind wounds crying for revenge,

[ANTISTROPHE 2]

Crying, tears and blood mingled.—Piteously born,
Those sons whose mother was of heavenly birth!
Her father was the god of the North Wind
30 And she was cradled by gales,
She raced with young colts on the glittering hills
And walked untrammeled in the open light:
But in her marriage deathless Fate found means
To build a tomb like yours for all her joy.

SCENE 5

[*Enter blind* TEIRESIAS, *led by a boy. The opening speeches of* TEIRESIAS *should be in singsong contrast to the realistic lines of* CREON.]

TEIRESIAS. This is the way the blind man comes,
Princes, Princes, Lock-step, two heads lit by the
eyes of one.

CREON. What new thing have you to tell us, old
Teiresias?

TEIRESIAS. I have much to tell you: listen to the
prophet, Creon.

5 **CREON.** I am not aware that I have ever failed to
listen.

TEIRESIAS. Then you have done wisely, King, and
ruled well.

CREON. I admit my debt to you.[12] But what have you
to say?

TEIRESIAS. This, Creon: you stand once more on the
edge of fate.

CREON. What do you mean? Your words are a kind of
dread.

---

11. Ares (er′ ēz′) god of war.

12. my debt to you Creon is admitting that he would not have acquired the
throne if Teiresias had not moved the former king, Oedipus, to undertake an
investigation that led eventually to his own downfall.

10   **TEIRESIAS.** Listen, Creon:

     I was sitting in my chair of augury,[13] at the place
     Where the birds gather about me. They were all
         a-chatter,
     As is their habit, when suddenly I heard
     A strange note in their jangling, a scream, a

15   Whirring fury; I knew that they were fighting,
     Tearing each other, dying
     In a whirlwind of wings clashing. And I was
         afraid.
     I began the rites of burnt-offering at the altar,
     But Hephaistos[14] failed me: instead of bright
         flame,

20   There was only the sputtering slime of the fat
         thigh-flesh
     Melting: the entrails dissolved in gray smoke,
     The bare bone burst from the welter. And no
         blaze!

     This was a sign from heaven. My boy described it,
     Seeing for me as I see for others.

25   I tell you, Creon, you yourself have brought
     This new calamity upon us. Our hearths and
         altars
     Are stained with the corruption of dogs and
         carrion birds
     That glut themselves on the corpse of Oedipus'
         son.
     The gods are deaf when we pray to them, their
         fire

30   Recoils from our offering, their birds of omen
     Have no cry of comfort, for they are gorged
     With the thick blood of the dead.
                          O my son,
     These are no trifles! Think: all men make mis
         takes,

35   But a good man yields when he knows his course
         is wrong,

---

13. chair of augury the seat near the temple from which Teiresias would deliver his predictions about the future. Augury is the practice of reading the future from omens, such as the flight of birds.

14. Hephaistos (hē fes′ təs) god of fire and the forge, who would be invoked, as he was by Teiresias, for aid in the starting of ceremonial fires.

TAKE NOTES

And repairs the evil. The only crime is pride.

Give in to the dead man, then: do not fight with a
    corpse—
What glory is it to kill a man who is dead?
Think, I beg you:
40 It is for your own good that I speak as I do.
You should be able to yield for your own good.

CREON. It seems that prophets have made me their
    especial province.
All my life long
I have been a kind of butt for the dull arrows
45 Of doddering fortunetellers!

                              No, Teiresias:

If your birds—if the great eagles of God
    himself
Should carry him stinking bit by bit to
    heaven,
I would not yield. I am not afraid of
    pollution:
50 No man can defile the gods.
                              Do what you will,

Go into business, make money,
    speculate
In India gold or that synthetic gold from
    Sardis,[15]
Get rich otherwise than by my consent to
    bury him.

55 Teiresias, it is a sorry thing when a wise
    man
Sells his wisdom, lets out his words for
    hire!

TEIRESIAS. Ah Creon! Is there no man left in the
    world—

CREON. To do what?—Come, let's have the
    aphorism![16]

TEIRESIAS. No man who knows that wisdom out
    weighs any wealth?

---

15. **Sardis** (sär′ dis) capital of ancient Lydia, which produced the first coins made
    from an alloy of gold and silver.
16. aphorism (af′ ə riz′ əm) *n.* brief saying. Creon is taunting the prophet and
    suggesting that the old man relies on profound-sounding expressions to make
    an impression.

60 **CREON.** As surely as bribes are baser than any
baseness.

TEIRESIAS. You are sick, Creon! You are deathly sick!

CREON. As you say: it is not my place to challenge a
prophet.

TEIRESIAS. Yet you have said my prophecy is for sale.

CREON. The generation of prophets has always loved
gold.

65 **TEIRESIAS.** The generation of kings has always loved
brass.

CREON. You forget yourself! You are speaking to your
King.

TEIRESIAS. I know it. You are a king because of me.

CREON. You have a certain skill; but you have sold
out.

TEIRESIAS. King, you will drive me to words that—

70 **CREON.**   Say them, say them!
Only remember: I will not pay you for them.

TEIRESIAS. No, you will find them too costly.

CREON.   No doubt. Speak:
Whatever you say, you will not change my will.

75 **TEIRESIAS.** Then take this, and take it to heart!
The time is not far off when you shall pay back
Corpse for corpse, flesh of your own flesh.
You have thrust the child of this world into living
night,
You have kept from the gods below the child that
is theirs:

80 The one in a grave before her death, the other,
Dead, denied the grave. This is your crime:
And the Furies[17] and the dark gods of Hell
Are swift with terrible punishment for you.

Do you want to buy me now, Creon?

---

17. Furies (fyoor´ ēz) goddesses of vengeance who punished those who committed
crimes against their own families.

TAKE NOTES

TAKE NOTES

85   Not many days,
And your house will be full of men and women
   weeping,
And curses will be hurled at you from far
Cities grieving for sons unburied, left to rot
Before the walls of Thebes.

90 These are my arrows, Creon: they are all for you.

[*To* BOY] But come, child: lead me home.
Let him waste his fine anger upon younger men.
Maybe he will learn at last
To control a wiser tongue in a better head.

                             [*Exit* TEIRESIAS.]

95 **CHORAGOS.** The old man has gone, King, but his
   words
Remain to plague us. I am old, too,
But I cannot remember that he was ever false.

CREON. That is true. . . . It troubles me.
Oh it is hard to give in! but it is worse

100 To risk everything for stubborn pride.

CHORAGOS. Creon: take my advice.

CREON.   What shall I do?

CHORAGOS. Go quickly: free Antigone from her vault
And build a tomb for the body of Polyneices.

105 **CREON.** You would have me do this?

CHORAGOS.   Creon, yes!
And it must be done at once: God moves
Swiftly to cancel the folly of stubborn men.

CREON. It is hard to deny the heart! But I
110 Will do it: I will not fight with destiny.

CHORAGOS. You must go yourself, you cannot leave it
   to others.

CREON. I will go.
           —Bring axes, servants:
Come with me to the tomb. I buried her, I
115 Will set her free.
            Oh quickly!
My mind misgives—

The laws of the gods are mighty, and a man must
  serve them
To the last day of his life!

[Exit CREON.]

Pæan

CHORAGOS.

God of many names   [STROPHE 1]

CHORUS.   O Iacchos[18]
                    son
of Kadmeian Semele[19]

5   O born of the Thunder!

Guardian of the West
                    Regent
of Eleusis' plain[20]
                    O Prince of maenad Thebes[21]
10   and the Dragon Field by rippling Ismenos:[22]

CHORAGOS.   [ANTISTROPHE 1]
God of many names

CHORUS.

                    the flame of torches

flares on our hills
                    the nymphs of Iacchos
15   dance at the spring of Castalia:[23]

from the vine-close mountain
                              come ah come in ivy:
Evohe evohe![24] sings through the streets of Thebes

CHORAGOS.   [STROPHE 2]
God of many names

---

18. **Iacchos** (ē′ ə kəs) one of several alternate names for Dionysos.
19. **Kadmeian Semele** (sem′ ə lē′) Semele was a mortal and the mother of
    Dionysos. She was the daughter of Thebes' founder, Kadmos.
20. **Eleusis'** (e loo′ sis əz) **plain** Located north of Athens, this plain was a site of
    worship for Dionysos and Demeter.
21. **maenad** (mē′ nad′) **Thebes** The city is here compared to a maenad, one
    of Dionysos' female worshipers. Such a follower would be thought of as
    uncontrolled or disturbed.
22. **Dragon Field . . . Ismenos** (is mē′ nas) The Dragon Field was located by the
    banks of Ismenos, a river near Thebes. Kadmos created warriors by sowing in
    the Dragon Field the teeth of the dragon he killed there.
23. **Castalia** (kas tā′ lē ə) location of a site sacred to Apollo.
24. **Evohe** (ē vō′ ē) triumphant shout of affirmation.

Antigone 143

TAKE NOTES

20 **CHORUS.**   Iacchos of Thebes
          heavenly Child
                    of Semele bride of the Thunderer!
          The shadow of plague is upon us:
                              come
25   with clement[25] feet
                    oh come from Parnasos[26]
          down the long slopes
                    across the lamenting water

CHORAGOS.   [ANTISTROPHE 2]
          Io[27] Fire! Chorister of the throbbing stars!
30   O purest among the voices of the night!
          Thou son of God, blaze for us!

CHORUS. Come with choric rapture of circling
          Maenads
          Who cry Io Iacche![28]
                    God of many names!

Exodus

                    [*Enter* MESSENGER, *left.*]

MESSENGER. Men of the line of Kadmos,[29] you who live
          Near Amphion's citadel:[30]
                    I cannot say
          Of any condition of human life "This is fixed,
5   This is clearly good, or bad." Fate raises up,
          And Fate casts down the happy and unhappy
             alike:
          No man can foretell his Fate.
                              Take the case of Creon:
          Creon was happy once, as I count happiness:
10   Victorious in battle, sole governor of the land,
          Fortunate father of children nobly born.
          And now it has all gone from him! Who can say
          That a man is still alive when his life's joy fails?
          He is a walking dead man. Grant him rich,

---

25. clement kind; favorable
26. Parnasos (pär nas´ əs) mountain that was sacred to both Dionysos and Apollo, located in central Greece.
27. Io (ē´ ō´) Greek word for "behold" or "hail."
28. Io Iacche (ē´ ō´ ē´ ə ke) cry of celebration used by Dionysian worshipers.
29. Kadmos (kad´ məs) founder of the city of Thebes, whose daughter, Semele, gave birth to Dionysos.
30. Amphion's (am fī´ ənz) citadel Amphion was a king of Thebes credited with erecting the walls of the fortress, or citadel, by using a magic lyre.

15   Let him live like a king in his great house:
      If his pleasure is gone, I would not give
      So much as the shadow of smoke for all he owns.

      Choragos. Your words hint at sorrow: what is your
          news for us?

      Messenger. They are dead. The living are guilty of
          their death.

20   **Choragos.** Who is guilty? Who is dead? Speak!

      Messenger.   Haimon.
          Haimon is dead; and the hand that killed him
          Is his own hand.

      Choragos.   His father's? or his own?

25   **Messenger.** His own, driven mad by the murder his
          father had done.

      Choragos. Teiresias, Teiresias, how clearly you saw
          it all!

      Messenger. This is my news: you must draw what
          conclusions you can from it.

      Choragos. But look: Eurydice, our Queen:
          Has she overheard us?

                    [*Enter* Eurydice *from the Palace, center.*]

30   **Eurydice.** I have heard something, friends:
          As I was unlocking the gate of Pallas'[31] shrine,
          For I needed her help today, I heard a voice
          Telling of some new sorrow. And I fainted
          There at the temple with all my maidens about me.
35   But speak again: whatever it is, I can bear it:
          Grief and I are no strangers.

      Messenger.   Dearest Lady,
          I will tell you plainly all that I have seen.
          I shall not try to comfort you: what is the use,
40   Since comfort could lie only in what is not true?
          The truth is always best.
                              I went with Creon
          To the outer plain where Polyneices was lying,
          No friend to pity him, his body shredded by dogs.

---

31. **Pallas'** (pal´ us oz) Pallas Athena, the goddess of wisdom.

TAKE NOTES

45 We made our prayers in that place to Hecate[32]
And Pluto,[33] that they would be merciful. And we bathed
The corpse with holy water, and we brought
Fresh-broken branches to burn what was left of it,
And upon the urn we heaped up a towering barrow
50 Of the earth of his own land.
                  When we were done, we ran
To the vault where Antigone lay on her couch of stone.
One of the servants had gone ahead,
And while he was yet far off he heard a voice
55 Grieving within the chamber, and he came back
And told Creon. And as the King went closer,
The air was full of wailing, the words lost,
And he begged us to make all haste. "Am I a prophet?"
He said, weeping, "And must I walk this road,
60 The saddest of all that I have gone before?
My son's voice calls me on. Oh quickly, quickly!
Look through the crevice there, and tell me
If it is Haimon, or some deception of the gods!"

We obeyed; and in the cavern's farthest corner
65 We saw her lying:
She had made a noose of her fine linen veil
And hanged herself. Haimon lay beside her,
His arms about her waist, lamenting her,
His love lost underground, crying out
70 That his father had stolen her away from him.

When Creon saw him the tears rushed to his eyes
And he called to him: "What have you done, child? Speak to me.
What are you thinking that makes your eyes so strange?
O my son, my son, I come to you on my knees!"

---

32. Hecate (hek′ ə tē) A goddess of the underworld, the resting place of dead souls in Greek mythology.

33. Pluto (pl′oo tō) Chief god of the underworld, who ruled the souls of the dead in Greek mythology.

75 But Haimon spat in his face. He said not a word,
Staring—
                    And suddenly drew his sword
And lunged. Creon shrank back, the blade
    missed; and the boy,
Desperate against himself, drove it half its length
80 Into his own side, and fell. And as he died
He gathered Antigone close in his arms again,
Choking, his blood bright red on her white cheek.
And now he lies dead with the dead, and she is his
At last, his bride in the houses of the dead.

> [*Exit* EURYDICE *into the Palace.*]

85 **CHORAGOS.** She has left us without a word. What can
    this mean?

MESSENGER. It troubles me, too; yet she knows what
    is best,
Her grief is too great for public lamentation,
And doubtless she has gone to her chamber to
    weep
For her dead son, leading her maidens in his
    dirge.

90 **CHORAGOS.** It may be so: but I fear this deep silence.

> [*Pause*]

MESSENGER. I will see what she is doing. I will go in.

> [*Exit* MESSENGER *into the Palace.*]

[*Enter* CREON *with attendants, bearing* HAIMON's *body.*]

CHORAGOS. But here is the King himself: oh look at
    him,
Bearing his own damnation in his arms.

CREON. Nothing you say can touch me any more.
95 My own blind heart has brought me
From darkness to final darkness. Here you see
The father murdering, the murdered son—
And all my civic wisdom!

Haimon my son, so young, so young to die,
100 I was the fool, not you; and you died for me.

CHORAGOS. That is the truth; but you were late in
    learning it.

CREON. This truth is hard to bear. Surely a god

TAKE NOTES

Has crushed me beneath the hugest weight of
   heaven,
And driven me headlong a barbaric way
105 To trample out the thing I held most dear.

The pains that men will take to come to pain!

[*Enter* MESSENGER *from the Palace.*]

MESSENGER. The burden you carry in your hands is
   heavy,
But it is not all: you will find more in your house.

CREON. What burden worse than this shall I find
   there?

110 MESSENGER. The Queen is dead.

CREON. O port of death, deaf world,
   Is there no pity for me? And you, Angel of evil,
   I was dead, and your words are death again.
   Is it true, boy? Can it be true?
115 Is my wife dead? Has death bred death?

MESSENGER. You can see for yourself.

[*The doors are opened, and the body of* EURYDICE *is
disclosed within.*]

CREON. Oh pity!
   All true, all true, and more than I can bear!
   O my wife, my son!

120 MESSENGER. She stood before the altar, and her heart
   Welcomed the knife her own hand guided,
   And a great cry burst from her lips for Megareus[34]
   dead,
   And for Haimon dead, her sons; and her last
   breath
   Was a curse for their father, the murderer of her
   sons.
125 And she fell, and the dark flowed in through her
   closing eyes.

CREON. O God, I am sick with fear.
   Are there no swords here? Has no one a blow for
   me?

---

34. Megareus (mə gaˊ rē əs) oldest son of Creon and Eurydice, who was killed in
the civil war by Argive forces invading Thebes.

Messenger. Her curse is upon you for the deaths of
both.

Creon. It is right that it should be. I alone am guilty.
130   I know it, and I say it. Lead me in,
        Quickly, friends.
        I have neither life nor substance. Lead me in.

Choragos. You are right, if there can be right in
        so much wrong.
        The briefest way is best in a world of sorrow.

135 **Creon.** Let it come,
        Let death come quickly, and be kind to me.
        I would not ever see the sun again.

Choragos. All that will come when it will; but we,
        meanwhile,
        Have much to do. Leave the future to itself.

140 **Creon.** All my heart was in that prayer!

Choragos. Then do not pray any more: the sky is
        deaf.

Creon. Lead me away. I have been rash and foolish.
        I have killed my son and my wife.
        I look for comfort; my comfort lies here dead.
145   Whatever my hands have touched has come to
            nothing.
        Fate has brought all my pride to a thought of
            dust.

[*As* Creon *is being led into the house, the* Choragos *advances
and speaks directly to the audience.*]

Choragos. There is no happiness where there is no
        wisdom;
        No wisdom but in submission to the gods.
        Big words are always punished,
150   And proud men in old age learn to be wise.

TAKE NOTES

TAKE NOTES

Games at Twilight

by Anita Desai

It was still too hot to play outdoors. They had had their tea, they had been washed and had their hair brushed, and after the long day of confinement in the house that was not cool but at least a protection from the sun, the children strained to get out. Their faces were red and bloated with the effort, but their mother would not open the door, everything was still curtained and shuttered in a way that stifled the children, made them feel that their lungs were stuffed with cotton wool and their noses with dust and if they didn't burst out into the light and see the sun and feel the air, they would choke.

"Please, Ma, please," they begged. "We'll play in the veranda and porch—we won't go a step out of the porch."

"You will, I know you will, and then—"

"No—we won't, we won't," they wailed so horrendously that she actually let down the bolt of the front door so that they burst out like seeds from a crackling, over-ripe pod into the veranda, with such wild, maniacal yells that she retreated to her bath and the shower of talcum powder and the fresh sari[1] that were to help her face the summer evening.

They faced the afternoon. It was too hot. Too bright. The white walls of the veranda glared stridently in the sun. The bougainvillea hung about it, purple and magenta, in livid balloons. The garden outside was like a tray made of beaten brass, flattened out on the red gravel and the stony soil in all shades of metal— aluminum, tin, copper and brass. No life stirred at this arid time of day—the birds still drooped, like dead fruit, in the papery tents of the trees; some squirrels lay limp on the wet earth under the garden tap. The outdoor dog lay stretched as if dead on the veranda

---

1. **sari** (sä´ rē) *n.* a long piece of cloth wrapped around the body, forming a skirt and draped over one shoulder; the traditional garment of Indian women.

mat, his paws and ears and tail all reaching out like dying travelers in search of water. He rolled his eyes at the children—two white marbles rolling in the purple sockets, begging for sympathy—and attempted to lift his tail in a wag but could not. It only twitched and lay still.

Then, perhaps roused by the shrieks of the children, a band of parrots suddenly fell out of the eucalyptus tree, tumbled frantically in the still, sizzling air, then sorted themselves out into battle formation and streaked away across the white sky.

The children, too, felt released. They too began tumbling, shoving, pushing against each other, frantic to start. Start what? Start their business. The business of the children's day which is—play.

"Let's play hide-and-seek."

"Who'll be It?"

"You be It."

"Why should I? You be—"

"You're the eldest—"

"That doesn't mean—"

The shoves became harder. Some kicked out. The motherly Mira intervened. She pulled the boys roughly apart. There was a tearing sound of cloth but it was lost in the heavy panting and angry grumbling and no one paid attention to the small sleeve hanging loosely off a shoulder.

"Make a circle, make a circle!" she shouted, firmly pulling and pushing till a kind of vague circle was formed. "Now clap!" she roared and, clapping, they all chanted in melancholy unison: "Dip, dip, dip—my blue ship—" and every now and then one or the other saw he was safe by the way his hands fell at the crucial moment—palm on palm, or back of hand on palm— and dropped out of the circle with a yell and a jump of relief and jubilation.

Raghu was It. He started to protest, to cry "You cheated—Mira cheated—Anu cheated—" but it was too late, the others had all already streaked away. There was no one to hear when he called out, "Only in the veranda—the porch—Ma said—Ma said to stay in the porch!" No one had stopped to listen, all he saw were their brown legs flashing through the dusty shrubs, scrambling up brick walls, leaping over compost heaps

TAKE NOTES

and hedges, and then the porch stood empty in the purple shade of the bougainvillea and the garden was as empty as before; even the limp squirrels had whisked away, leaving everything gleaming, brassy and bare.

Only small Manu suddenly reappeared, as if he had dropped out of an invisible cloud or from a bird's claws, and stood for a moment in the center of the yellow lawn, chewing his finger and near to tears as he heard Raghu shouting, with his head pressed against the veranda wall, "Eighty-three, eighty-five, eighty-nine, ninety . . ." and then made off in a panic, half of him wanting to fly north, the other half counseling south. Raghu turned just in time to see the flash of his white shorts and the uncertain skittering of his red sandals, and charged after him with such a bloodcurdling yell that Manu stumbled over the hosepipe, fell into its rubber coils and lay there weeping, "I won't be It—you have to find them all—all—All!"

"I know I have to, idiot," Raghu said, superciliously[2] kicking him with his toe. "You're dead," he said with satisfaction, licking the beads of perspiration off his upper lip, and then stalked off in search of worthier prey, whistling spiritedly so that the hiders should hear and tremble.

Ravi heard the whistling and picked his nose in a panic, trying to find comfort by burrowing the finger deep—deep into that soft tunnel. He felt himself too exposed, sitting on an upturned flower pot behind the garage. Where could he burrow? He could run around the garage if he heard Raghu come—around and around and around—but he hadn't much faith in his short legs when matched against Raghu's long, hefty, hairy footballer legs. Ravi had a frightening glimpse of them as Raghu combed the hedge of crotons and hibiscus, trampling delicate ferns underfoot as he did so. Ravi looked about him desperately, swallowing a small ball of snot in his fear.

The garage was locked with a great heavy lock to which the driver had the key in his room, hanging

---

2. **superciliously** (sōō′ pər sil′ ē əs lē) *adv.* haughtily; in a manner expressing pride in oneself and scorn for the other person.

from a nail on the wall under his work-shirt. Ravi had peeped in and seen him still sprawling on his string-cot in his vest and striped underpants, the hair on his chest and the hair in his nose shaking with the vibrations of his phlegm-obstructed snores. Ravi had wished he were tall enough, big enough to reach the key on the nail, but it was impossible, beyond his reach for years to come. He had sidled away and sat dejectedly on the flower pot. That at least was cut to his own size.

But next to the garage was another shed with a big green door. Also locked. No one even knew who had the key to the lock. That shed wasn't opened more than once a year when Ma turned out all the old broken bits of furniture and rolls of matting and leaking buckets, and the white ant hills were broken and swept away and Flit sprayed into the spider webs and rat holes so that the whole operation was like the looting of a poor, ruined and conquered city. The green leaves of the door sagged. They were nearly off their rusty hinges. The hinges were large and made a small gap between the door and the walls—only just large enough for rats, dogs, and, possibly, Ravi to slip through.

Ravi had never cared to enter such a dark and depressing mortuary of defunct household goods seething with such unspeakable and alarming animal life but, as Raghu's whistling grew angrier and sharper and his crashing and storming in the hedge wilder, Ravi suddenly slipped off the flower pot and through the crack and was gone. He chuckled aloud with astonishment at his own temerity[3] so that Raghu came out of the hedge, stood silent with his hands on his hips, listening, and finally shouted "I heard you! I'm coming! Got you—" and came charging round the garage only to find the upturned flower pot, the yellow dust, the crawling of white ants in a mud-hill against the closed shed door—nothing. Snarling, he bent to pick up a stick and went off, whacking it against the garage and shed walls as if to beat out his prey.

Ravi shook, then shivered with delight, with self-congratulation. Also with fear. It was dark, spooky in

---

3. temerity (tə mer´ ə tē) *n.* recklessness; foolish boldness.

TAKE NOTES

the shed. It had a muffled smell, as of graves. Ravi had once got locked into the linen cupboard and sat there weeping for half an hour before he was rescued. But at least that had been a familiar place, and even smelled pleasantly of starch, laundry and, reassuringly, of his mother. But the shed smelled of rats, ant hills, dust and spider webs. Also of less definable, less recognizable horrors. And it was dark. Except for the white-hot cracks along the door, there was no light. The roof was very low. Although Ravi was small, he felt as if he could reach up and touch it with his finger tips. But he didn't stretch. He hunched himself into a ball so as not to bump into anything, touch or feel anything. What might there not be to touch him and feel him as he stood there, trying to see in the dark? Something cold, or slimy—like a snake. Snakes! He leapt up as Raghu whacked the wall with his stick—then quickly realizing what it was, felt almost relieved to hear Raghu, hear his stick. It made him feel protected.

But Raghu soon moved away. There wasn't a sound once his footsteps had gone around the garage and disappeared. Ravi stood frozen inside the shed. Then he shivered all over. Something had tickled the back of his neck. It took him a while to pick up the courage to lift his hand and explore. It was an insect—perhaps a spider—exploring him. He squashed it and wondered how many more creatures were watching him, waiting to reach out and touch him, the stranger.

There was nothing now. After standing in that position—his hand still on his neck, feeling the wet splodge of the squashed spider gradually dry—for minutes, hours, his legs began to tremble with the effort, the inaction. By now he could see enough in the dark to make out the large solid shapes of old wardrobes, broken buckets and bedsteads piled on top of each other around him. He recognized an old bathtub—patches of enamel glimmered at him and at last he lowered himself onto its edge.

He contemplated slipping out of the shed and into the fray. He wondered if it would not be better to be captured by Raghu and be returned to the milling crowd as long as he could be in the sun, the light, the free spaces of the garden and the familiarity of his brothers, sisters and cousins. It would be evening soon. Their games would become legitimate. The parents would sit out on the lawn on cane basket chairs and watch them as they tore around the garden or gathered in knots to share a loot of mulberries or black, teeth-splitting jamun from the garden trees. The gardener would fix the hosepipe to the water tap and water would fall lavishly through the air to the ground, soaking the dry yellow grass and the red gravel and arousing the sweet, the intoxicating scent of water on dry earth—that loveliest scent in the world. Ravi sniffed for a whiff of it. He half-rose from the bathtub, then heard the despairing scream of one of the girls as Raghu bore down upon her. There was the sound of a crash, and of rolling about in the bushes, the shrubs, then screams and accusing sobs of, "I touched the den—" "You did not—" "I did—" "You liar, you did not" and then a fading away and silence again.

Ravi sat back on the harsh edge of the tub, deciding to hold out a bit longer. What fun if they were all found and caught—he alone left unconquered! He had never known that sensation. Nothing more wonderful had ever happened to him than being taken out by an uncle and bought a whole slab of chocolate all to himself, or being flung into the soda-man's pony cart and driven up to the gate by the friendly driver with the red beard and pointed ears. To defeat Raghu—that hirsute,[4] hoarse-voiced football champion—and to be the winner in a circle of older, bigger, luckier children— that would be thrilling beyond imagination. He hugged his knees together and smiled to himself almost shyly at the thought of so much victory, such laurels.[5]

There he sat smiling, knocking his heels against the bathtub, now and then getting up and going to the door to put his ear to the broad crack and listening for sounds of the game, the pursuer and the pursued, and then returning to his seat with the dogged determination of the true winner, a breaker of records, a champion.

It grew darker in the shed as the light at the door grew softer, fuzzier, turned to a kind of crumbling

---

4. **hirsute** (hɦr′ so͞ot′) *adj.* hairy.
5. **laurels** (lôr′ əlz) *n.* leaves of the laurel tree; worn in a crown as an ancient symbol of victory in a contest.

TAKE NOTES

yellow pollen that turned to yellow fur, blue fur, gray fur. Evening. Twilight. The sound of water gushing, falling. The scent of earth receiving water, slaking its thirst in great gulps and releasing that green scent of freshness, coolness. Through the crack Ravi saw the long purple shadows of the shed and the garage lying still across the yard. Beyond that, the white walls of the house. The bougainvillea had lost its lividity, hung in dark bundles that quaked and twittered and seethed with masses of homing sparrows. The lawn was shut off from his view. Could he hear the children's voices? It seemed to him that he could. It seemed to him that he could hear them chanting, singing, laughing. But what about the game? What had happened? Could it be over? How could it when he was still not found?

It then occurred to him that he could have slipped out long ago, dashed across the yard to the veranda and touched the "den." It was necessary to do that to win. He had forgotten. He had only remembered the part of hiding and trying to elude the seeker. He had done that so successfully, his success had occupied him so wholly that he had quite forgotten that success had to be clinched by that final dash to victory and the ringing cry of "Den!"

With a whimper he burst through the crack, fell on his knees, got up and stumbled on stiff, benumbed legs across the shadowy yard, crying heartily by the time he reached the veranda so that when he flung himself at the white pillar and bawled, "Den! Den! Den!" his voice broke with rage and pity at the disgrace of it all and he felt himself flooded with tears and misery.

Out on the lawn, the children stopped chanting. They all turned to stare at him in amazement. Their faces were pale and triangular in the dusk. The trees and bushes around them stood inky and sepulchral,[6] spilling long shadows across them. They stared, wondering at his reappearance, his passion, his wild animal howling. Their mother rose from her basket chair and came toward him, worried, annoyed, saying, "Stop it, stop it, Ravi. Don't be a baby. Have you hurt yourself?" Seeing him attended to, the children went

---

6. **sepulchral** (sə pul′ krəl) *adj.* of the tomb; gloomy.

back to clasping their hands and chanting "The grass
is green, the rose is red. . . . "

But Ravi would not let them. He tore himself out of
his mother's grasp and pounded across the lawn into
their midst, charging at them with his head lowered so
that they scattered in surprise. "I won, I won, I won,"
he bawled, shaking his head so that the big tears flew.
"Raghu didn't find me. I won, I won—"

It took them a minute to grasp what he was saying,
even who he was. They had quite forgotten him. Raghu
had found all the others long ago. There had been a
fight about who was to be It next. It had been so fierce
that their mother had emerged from her bath and
made them change to another game. Then they had
played another and another. Broken mulberries from
the tree and eaten them. Helped the driver wash the
car when their father returned from work. Helped the
gardener water the beds till he roared at them and
swore he would complain to their parents. The parents
had come out, taken up their positions on the cane
chairs. They had begun to play again, sing and chant.
All this time no one had remembered Ravi. Having
disappeared from the scene, he had disappeared from
their minds. Clean.

"Don't be a fool," Raghu said roughly, pushing him
aside, and even Mira said, "Stop howling, Ravi. If you
want to play, you can stand at the end of the line," and
she put him there very firmly.

The game proceeded. Two pairs of arms reached up
and met in an arc. The children trooped under it again
and again in a lugubrious[7] circle, ducking their heads
and intoning

"The grass is green,
The rose is red;
Remember me
When I am dead, dead, dead, dead . . ."

And the arc of thin arms trembled in the twilight,
and the heads were bowed so sadly, and their feet
tramped to that melancholy refrain so mournfully,
so helplessly, that Ravi could not bear it. He would

---

7. lugubrious (lə g$\overline{oo}$´ brē əs) *adj.* very sad, especially in an exaggerated or
ridiculous way.

TAKE NOTES

not follow them, he would not be included in this funereal game. He had wanted victory and triumph—not a funeral. But he had been forgotten, left out and he would not join them now. The ignominy[8] of being forgotten—how could he face it? He felt his heart go heavy and ache inside him unbearably. He lay down full length on the damp grass, crushing his face into it, no longer crying, silenced by a terrible sense of his insignificance.

---

8. **ignominy** (ig´ nə min´ ē) *n.* shame and dishonor.

Prometheus and the First People

by Olivia E. Coolidge

Humanity's Beginnings

The Greeks have several stories about how man came to be. One declares that he was created in the age of Kronos,[1] or Saturn, who ruled before Zeus [zo͞os]. At that time, the legend says, there was no sorrow, toil, sickness, or age. Men lived their lives in plenty and died as though they went to sleep. They tilled[2] no ground, built no cities, killed no living thing, and among them war was unknown. The earth brought forth strawberries, cherries, and ears of wheat for them. Even on the bramble bushes grew berries good to eat. Milk and sweet nectar flowed in rivers for men to drink, and honey dripped from hollow trees. Men lived in caves and thickets, needing little shelter, for the season was always spring.

Another legend declares that Zeus conceived of animals first and he entrusted their creation to Prometheus [prō mē′ thē əs] and Epimetheus [ep ə mē′ thē əs], his brother. First, Epimetheus undertook to order all things, but he was a heedless person and soon got into trouble. Finally he was forced to appeal to Prometheus.

"What have you done?" asked Prometheus.

"Down on the earth," answered his brother, "there is a green, grassy clearing, ringed by tall oak trees and shaded by steep slopes from all but the midday sun. There I sat and the animals came to me, while I gave to each the gifts which should be his from this time forward. Air I gave to the birds, seas to the fishes, land to four-footed creatures and the creeping insects, and to some, like the moles, I gave burrows beneath the earth."

"That was well done," answered Prometheus. "What else did you do?"

---

1. Kronos (krō′ nəs) son of the sky and the earth; father of Zeus.
2. tilled v. cultivated; plowed or hoed.

TAKE NOTES

"Strength," said Epimetheus, "I gave to lions and tigers, and the fierce animals of the woods. Size I gave to others like the great whales of the sea. The deer I made swift and timid, and the insects I made tiny that they might escape from sight. I gave warm fur to the great bears and the little squirrels, keen eyes and sharp talons[3] to the birds of prey, tusks to the elephant, hide to the wild boar, sweet songs and bright feathers to the birds. To each I gave some special excellence, that whether large or small, kind or terrible, each might live in his own place, find food, escape enemies, and enjoy the wide world which is his to inhabit."

"All this is very good," said his brother, Prometheus. "You have done well. Wherein lies your trouble?"

"Because I did not think it out beforehand," said the heedless brother sadly, "I did not count how many animals there were to be before I started giving. Now when I have given all, there comes one last animal for whom I have neither skill nor shape, nor any place to dwell in. Everything has been given already."

"What is this animal," said Prometheus, "who has been forgotten?"

"His name," said Epimetheus, "is Man."

Thus it was that the future of man was left to Prometheus, who was forced to make man different from all other creatures. Therefore he gave him the shape of the gods themselves and the privilege of walking upright as they do. He gave him no special home, but made him ruler over the whole earth, and over the sea and air. Finally, he gave him no special strength or swiftness, but stole a spark from heaven and lighted a heavenly fire within his mind which should teach him to understand, to count, to speak, to remember. Man learned from it how to build cities, tame animals, raise crops, build boats, and do all the things that animals cannot. Prometheus also kindled fire on earth that man might smelt[4] metals and make tools. In fact, from this heavenly fire of Prometheus all man's greatness comes.

Before this time fire was a divine thing and belonged only to the gods. It was one of their greatest treasures,

---

3. **talons** (tal´ enz) *n.* claws (of birds of prey).
4. **smelt** *v.* purify metal by melting it.

and Zeus would never have given Prometheus permission to use it in the creation of man. Therefore when Prometheus stole it, Zeus was furious indeed. He chained Prometheus to a great, lofty rock, where the sun scorched him by day and the cruel frost tortured him by night. Not content with that, he sent an eagle to tear him, so that, though he could not die, he lived in agony. For many centuries Prometheus hung in torment, but he was wiser than Zeus, and by reason of a secret he had, he forced Zeus in later ages to set him free. By then, also, Zeus had learned that there is more in ruling than power and cruelty. Thus, the two at last were friends. •

The Coming of Evil

After the punishment of Prometheus, Zeus planned to take his revenge on man. He could not recall the gift of fire, since it had been given by one of the immortals,[5] but he was not content that man should possess this treasure in peace and become perhaps as great as were the gods themselves. He therefore took counsel with the other gods, and together they made for man a woman. All the gods gave gifts to this new creation. Aphrodite [af´ rə dīt´ ē] gave her fresh beauty like the spring itself. The goddess Athene [ə thē´ nē] dressed her and put on her a garland of flowers and green leaves. She had also a golden diadem[6] beautifully decorated with figures of animals. In her heart Hermes [hʉr´ mēz´] put cunning, deceit, and curiosity. She was named Pandora [pan dôr´ ə], which means All-Gifted, since each of the gods had given her something. The last gift was a chest in which there was supposed to be great treasure, but which Pandora was instructed never to open. Then Hermes, the Messenger, took the girl and brought her to Epimetheus.

Epimetheus had been warned by his brother to receive no gifts from Zeus, but he was a heedless person, as ever, and Pandora was very lovely. He accepted her, therefore, and for a while they lived together in happiness, for Pandora besides her beauty had been given both wit and charm. Eventually,

---

5. **immortals** (i môrt´ ′lz) *n.* those who do not die.
6. **diadem** (dī´ ə dem´) *n.* crown.

TAKE NOTES

however, her curiosity got the better of her, and she determined to see for herself what treasure it was that the gods had given her. One day when she was alone, she went over to the corner where her chest lay and cautiously lifted the lid for a peep. The lid flew up out of her hands and knocked her aside, while before her frightened eyes dreadful, shadowy shapes flew out of the box in an endless stream. There were hunger, disease, war, greed, anger, jealousy, toil, and all the griefs and hardships to which man from that day has been subject. Each was terrible in appearance, and as it passed, Pandora saw something of the misery that her thoughtless action had brought on her descendants. At last the stream slackened,[7] and Pandora, who had been paralyzed with fear and horror, found strength to shut her box. The only thing left in it now, however, was the one good gift the gods had put in among so many evil ones. This was hope, and since that time the hope that is in man's heart is the only thing which has made him able to bear the sorrows that Pandora brought upon him.

The Great Flood

When evil first came among mankind, people became very wicked. War, robbery, treachery, and murder prevailed throughout the world. Even the worship of the gods, the laws of truth and honor, reverence[8] for parents and brotherly love were neglected.

Finally, Zeus determined to destroy the race of men altogether, and the other gods agreed. All the winds were therefore shut up in a cave except the South Wind, the wet one. He raced over the earth with water streaming from his beard and long, white hair. Clouds gathered around his head, and dew dripped from his wings and the ends of his garments. With him went Iris, the rainbow goddess, while below Poseidon [pō sī´ dən] smote the earth with his trident until it shook and gaped open, so that the waters of the sea rushed up over the land.

Fields and farmhouses were buried. Fish swam in the tops of the trees. Sea beasts were quietly feeding

---

7. **slackened** (slak´ ənd) v. diminished; became less active.
8. **reverence** (rev´ ə rəns) n. feeling or display of great respect.

where flocks and herds had grazed before. On the surface of the water, boars, stags, lions, and tigers struggled desperately to keep afloat. Wolves swam in the midst of flocks of sheep, but the sheep were not frightened by them, and the wolves never thought of their natural prey. Each fought for his own life and forgot the others. Over them wheeled countless birds, winging far and wide in the hope of finding something to rest upon. Eventually they too fell into the water and were drowned.

All over the water were men in small boats or makeshift rafts. Some even had oars which they tried to use, but the waters were fierce and stormy, and there was nowhere to go. In time all were drowned, until at last there was no one left but an old man and his wife, Deucalion [dōō kāl′ ē ən] and Pyrrha [pir′ ə]. These two people had lived in truth and justice, unlike the rest of mankind. They had been warned of the coming of the flood and had built a boat and stocked it. For nine days and nights they floated until Zeus took pity on them and they came to the top of Mount Parnassus, the sacred home of the Muses.[9] There they found land and disembarked to wait while the gods recalled the water they had unloosed.

When the waters fell, Deucalion and Pyrrha looked over the land, despairing. Mud and sea slime covered the earth; all living things had been swept away. Slowly and sadly they made their way down the mountain until they came to a temple where there had been an oracle.[10] Black seaweed dripped from the pillars now, and the mud was over all. Nevertheless the two knelt down and kissed the temple steps while Deucalion prayed to the goddess to tell them what they should do. All men were dead but themselves, and they were old. It was impossible that they should have children to people the earth again. Out of the temple a great voice was heard speaking strange words.

"Depart," it said, "with veiled heads and loosened robes, and throw behind you as you go the bones of your mother."

---

9. **Muses** (myōōz′ ez) *n.* nine goddesses who rule over literature and the arts and sciences.
10. **oracle** (ôr′ ə kəl) *n.* person who, when consulted on a matter, is said to reveal the will of the gods.

TAKE NOTES

Pyrrha was in despair when she heard this saying. "The bones of our mother!" she cried. "How can we tell now where they lie? Even if we knew, we could never do such a dreadful thing as to disturb their resting place and scatter them over the earth like an armful of stones."

"Stones!" said Deucalion quickly. "That must be what the goddess means. After all Earth is our mother, and the other thing is too horrible for us to suppose that a goddess would ever command it."

Accordingly both picked up armfuls of stones, and as they went away from the temple with faces veiled, they cast the stones behind them. From each of those Deucalion cast sprang up a man, and from Pyrrha's stones sprang women. Thus the earth was repeopled, and in the course of time it brought forth again animals from itself, and all was as before. Only from that time men have been less sensitive and have found it easier to endure toil, and sorrow, and pain, since now they are descended from stones.

from Sundiata: An Epic of Old Mali

by D. T. Niane

Characters in Sundiata

Balla Fasséké (bä´ lä fä sä´ kä): Griot and counselor of Sundiata

Boukari (bo͞o kä´ rē): Son of the king and Namandjé, one of his wives; also called Manding (män´ diŋ) Boukari

Dankaran Touman (dän´ kä rän to͞o´ män): Son of the king and his first wife, Sassouma, who is also called Sassouma Bérété

Djamarou (jä mä´ ro͞o): Daughter of Sogolon and the king; sister of Sundiata and Kolonkan

Farakourou (fä rä ko͞o´ ro͞o): Master of the forges

Gnankouman Doua (nän ko͞o´ män do͞o´ ə): The king's griot; also called, simply, Doua

Kolonkan (kō lōn´ kən): Sundiata's eldest sister

Namandjé (nä män´ jē): One of the king's wives

Naré Maghan (nä´ rä mäg´ hän): Sundiata's father; the king of Mali before Sundiata

Nounfaïri (no͞on´ fä ē´ rē): Soothsayer and smith; father of Farakourou

Sassouma Bérété (sä so͞o´ mä be´ re te): The king's first wife

Sogolon (sô gô lōn´): Sundiata's mother; also called Sogolon Kedjou (kā´ jo͞o)

Sundiata (so͞on dyä´ tä): Legendary king of Mali; referred to as Djata (dyä´ tä) and Sogolon Djata ("son of Sogolon"), and Mari (mä´ rē) Djata.

TAKE NOTES

TAKE NOTES

Childhood

God has his mysteries which none can fathom. You, perhaps, will be a king. You can do nothing about it. You, on the other hand, will be unlucky, but you can do nothing about that either. Each man finds his way already marked out for him and he can change nothing of it.

Sogolon's son had a slow and difficult childhood. At the age of three he still crawled along on all-fours while children of the same age were already walking. He had nothing of the great beauty of his father Naré Maghan. He had a head so big that he seemed unable to support it; he also had large eyes which would open wide whenever anyone entered his mother's house. He was taciturn[1] and used to spend the whole day just sitting in the middle of the house. Whenever his mother went out he would crawl on all-fours to rummage about in the calabashes[2] in search of food, for he was very greedy.

Malicious tongues began to blab. What three-year-old has not yet taken his first steps? What three-year-old is not the despair of his parents through his whims and shifts of mood? What three-year-old is not the joy of his circle through his backwardness in talking? Sogolon Djata (for it was thus that they called him, prefixing his mother's name to his), Sogolon Djata, then, was very different from others of his own age. He spoke little and his severe face never relaxed into a smile. You would have thought that he was already thinking, and what amused children of his age bored him. Often Sogolon would make some of them come to him to keep him company. These children were already walking and she hoped that Djata, seeing his companions walking, would be tempted to do likewise. But nothing came of it. Besides, Sogolon Djata would brain the poor little things with his already strong arms and none of them would come near him any more.

The king's first wife was the first to rejoice at Sogolon Djata's infirmity. Her own son, Dankaran Touman,

---

1. **taciturn** (tasʹ ə tʉrnʹ) *adj.* almost always silent; not liking to talk.
2. **calabashes** (kalʹ ə bashʹ əz) *n.* dried, hollow shells of gourds (squashlike fruits), used as bowls, cups, and so on.

was already eleven. He was a fine and lively boy, who spent the day running about the village with those of his own age. He had even begun his initiation in the bush.[3] The king had had a bow made for him and he used to go behind the town to practice archery with his companions. Sassouma was quite happy and snapped her fingers at Sogolon, whose child was still crawling on the ground. Whenever the latter happened to pass by her house, she would say, "Come, my son, walk, jump, leap about. The jinn didn't promise you anything out of the ordinary,[4] but I prefer a son who walks on his two legs to a lion that crawls on the ground." She spoke thus whenever Sogolon went by her door. The innuendo would go straight home and then she would burst into laughter, that diabolical laughter which a jealous woman knows how to use so well.

Her son's infirmity weighed heavily upon Sogolon Kedjou; she had resorted to all her talent as a sorceress to give strength to her son's legs, but the rarest herbs had been useless. The king himself lost hope.

How impatient man is! Naré Maghan became imperceptibly estranged but Gnankouman Doua never ceased reminding him of the hunter's words. Sogolon became pregnant again. The king hoped for a son, but it was a daughter called Kolonkan. She resembled her mother and had nothing of her father's beauty. The disheartened king debarred Sogolon from his house and she lived in semi-disgrace for a while. Naré Maghan married the daughter of one of his allies, the king of the Kamaras. She was called Namandjé and her beauty was legendary. A year later she brought a boy into the world. When the king consulted soothsayers[5] on the destiny of this son he received the reply that Namandjé's child would be the right hand of some mighty king. The king gave the newly-born the name of Boukari. He was to be called Manding Boukari or Manding Bory later on.

---

3. **initiation in the bush** education in tribal lore given to twelve-year-old West African boys so they can become full members of the tribe.
4. **The jinn . . . ordinary** Jinn are supernatural beings said to influence human affairs. They promised that the son of Sogolon would make Mali a great empire.
5. **soothsayers** (sōōth′ sā′ erz) *n.* people who profess to foretell the future.

Naré Maghan was very perplexed. Could it be that the stiff-jointed son of Sogolon was the one the hunter soothsayer had foretold?

"The Almighty has his mysteries," Gnankouman Doua would say and, taking up the hunter's words, added, "The silk-cotton tree emerges from a tiny seed."

One day Naré Maghan came along to the house of Nounfaïri, the blacksmith seer of Niani. He was an old, blind man. He received the king in the anteroom which served as his workshop. To the king's question he replied, "When the seed germinates growth is not always easy; great trees grow slowly but they plunge their roots deep into the ground."

"But has the seed really germinated?" said the king.

"Of course," replied the blind seer. "Only the growth is not as quick as you would like it; how impatient man is."

This interview and Doua's confidence gave the king some assurance. To the great displeasure of Sassouma Bérété the king restored Sogolon to favor and soon another daughter was born to her. She was given the name of Djamarou.

However, all Niani talked of nothing else but the stiff-legged son of Sogolon. He was now seven and he still crawled to get about. In spite of all the king's affection, Sogolon was in despair. Naré Maghan aged and he felt his time coming to an end. Dankaran Touman, the son of Sassouma Bérété, was now a fine youth.

One day Naré Maghan made Mari Djata come to him and he spoke to the child as one speaks to an adult. "Mari Djata, I am growing old and soon I shall be no more among you, but before death takes me off I am going to give you the present each king gives his successor. In Mali every prince has his own griot. Doua's father was my father's griot, Doua is mine and the son of Doua, Balla Fasséké here, will be your griot. Be inseparable friends from this day forward. From his mouth you will hear the history of your ancestors, you will learn the art of governing Mali according to the principles which our ancestors have bequeathed to us. I have served my term and done my duty too. I have done everything which a king of Mali ought to do. I am handing an enlarged kingdom over to you and I leave you sure allies. May your destiny be accomplished, but never forget that Niani is your capital and Mali the cradle of your ancestors."

The child, as if he had understood the whole meaning of the king's words, beckoned Balla Fasséké to approach. He made room for him on the hide he was sitting on and then said, "Balla, you will be my griot."

"Yes, son of Sogolon, if it pleases God," replied Balla Fasséké.

The king and Doua exchanged glances that radiated confidence. •

The Lion's Awakening

A short while after this interview between Naré Maghan and his son the king died.

Sogolon's son was no more than seven years old. The council of elders met in the king's palace. It was no use Doua's defending the king's will which reserved the throne for Mari Djata, for the council took no account of Naré Maghan's wish. With the help of Sassouma Bérété's intrigues, Dankaran Touman was proclaimed king and a regency council[6] was formed in which the queen mother was all-powerful. A short time after, Doua died.

As men have short memories, Sogolon's son was spoken of with nothing but irony and scorn. People had seen one-eyed kings, one-armed kings, and lame kings, but a stiff-legged king had never been heard tell of. No matter how great the destiny promised for Mari Djata might be, the throne could not be given to someone who had no power in his legs; if the jinn loved him, let them begin by giving him the use of his legs. Such were the remarks that Sogolon heard every day. The queen mother, Sassouma Bérété, was the source of all this gossip.

Having become all-powerful, Sassouma Bérété persecuted Sogolon because the late Naré Maghan had preferred her. She banished Sogolon and her son to a back yard of the palace. Mari Djata's mother now

---

6. **regency** (rē´ jən sē) **council** group that rules instead of the king or queen when the king or queen is still a child or is otherwise incapable of ruling.

TAKE NOTES

occupied an old hut which had served as a lumber-room of Sassouma's.

The wicked queen mother allowed free passage to all those inquisitive people who wanted to see the child that still crawled at the age of seven. Nearly all the inhabitants of Niani filed into the palace and the poor Sogolon wept to see herself thus given over to public ridicule. Mari Djata took on a ferocious look in front of the crowd of sightseers. Sogolon found a little consolation only in the love of her eldest daughter, Kolonkan. She was four and she could walk. She seemed to understand all her mother's miseries and already she helped her with the housework. Sometimes, when Sogolon was attending to the chores, it was she who stayed beside her sister Djamarou, quite small as yet.

Sogolon Kedjou and her children lived on the queen mother's leftovers, but she kept a little garden in the open ground behind the village. It was there that she passed her brightest moments looking after her onions and gnougous.[7] One day she happened to be short of condiments and went to the queen mother to beg a little baobab leaf.[8]

"Look you," said the malicious Sassouma, "I have a calabash full. Help yourself, you poor woman. As for me, my son knew how to walk at seven and it was he who went and picked these baobab leaves. Take them then, since your son is unequal to mine." Then she laughed derisively with that fierce laughter which cuts through your flesh and penetrates right to the bone.

Sogolon Kedjou was dumbfounded. She had never imagined that hate could be so strong in a human being. With a lump in her throat she left Sassouma's. Outside her hut Mari Djata, sitting on his useless legs, was blandly eating out of a calabash. Unable to contain herself any longer, Sogolon burst into sobs and seizing a piece of wood, hit her son.

"Oh son of misfortune, will you never walk? Through your fault I have just suffered the greatest affront of my life! What have I done, God, for you to punish me in this way?"

---

7. **gnougous** (n$\overline{oo}$′ g$\overline{oo}$z′) *n.* root vegetables.
8. **baobab** (bā′ ō bab′) **leaf** The baobab is a thick-trunked tree; its leaves are used to flavor foods.

Mari Djata seized the piece of wood and, looking at his mother, said, "Mother, what's the matter?"

"Shut up, nothing can ever wash me clean of this insult."

"But what then?"

"Sassouma has just humiliated me over a matter of a baobab leaf. At your age her own son could walk and used to bring his mother baobab leaves."

"Cheer up, Mother, cheer up."

"No. It's too much. I can't."

"Very well then, I am going to walk today," said Mari Djata. "Go and tell my father's smiths to make me the heaviest possible iron rod. Mother, do you want just the leaves of the baobab or would you rather I brought you the whole tree?"

"Ah, my son, to wipe out this insult I want the tree and its roots at my feet outside my hut."

Balla Fasséké, who was present, ran to the master smith, Farakourou, to order an iron rod.

Sogolon had sat down in front of her hut. She was weeping softly and holding her head between her two hands. Mari Djata went calmly back to his calabash of rice and began eating again as if nothing had happened. From time to time he looked up discreetly at his mother who was murmuring in a low voice, "I want the whole tree, in front of my hut, the whole tree."

All of a sudden a voice burst into laughter behind the hut. It was the wicked Sassouma telling one of her serving women about the scene of humiliation and she was laughing loudly so that Sogolon could hear. Sogolon fled into the hut and hid her face under the blankets so as not to have before her eyes this heedless boy, who was more preoccupied with eating than with anything else. With her head buried in the bedclothes Sogolon wept and her body shook violently. Her daughter, Sogolon Djamarou, had come and sat down beside her and she said, "Mother, Mother, don't cry. Why are you crying?"

Mari Djata had finished eating and, dragging himself along on his legs, he came and sat under the wall of the hut for the sun was scorching. What was he thinking about? He alone knew. •

The royal forges were situated outside the walls and over a hundred smiths worked there. The bows,

TAKE NOTES

spears, arrows and shields of Niani's warriors came from there. When Balla Fasséké came to order the iron rod, Farakourou said to him, "The great day has arrived then?"

"Yes. Today is a day like any other, but it will see what no other day has seen."

The master of the forges, Farakourou, was the son of the old Nounfaïri, and he was a soothsayer like his father. In his workshops there was an enormous iron bar wrought by his father, Nounfaïri. Everybody wondered what this bar was destined to be used for. Farakourou called six of his apprentices and told them to carry the iron bar to Sogolon's house.

When the smiths put the gigantic iron bar down in front of the hut the noise was so frightening that Sogolon, who was lying down, jumped up with a start. Then Balla Fasséké, son of Gnankouman Doua, spoke.

"Here is the great day, Mari Djata. I am speaking to you, Maghan, son of Sogolon. The waters of the Niger can efface the stain from the body, but they cannot wipe out an insult. Arise, young lion, roar, and may the bush know that from henceforth it has a master."

The apprentice smiths were still there, Sogolon had come out and everyone was watching Mari Djata. He crept on all-fours and came to the iron bar. Supporting himself on his knees and one hand, with the other hand he picked up the iron bar without any effort and stood it up vertically. Now he was resting on nothing but his knees and held the bar with both his hands. A deathly silence had gripped all those present. Sogolon Djata closed his eyes, held tight, the muscles in his arms tensed. With a violent jerk he threw his weight on to it and his knees left the ground. Sogolon Kedjou was all eyes and watched her son's legs which were trembling as though from an electric shock. Djata was sweating and the sweat ran from his brow. In a great effort he straightened up and was on his feet at one go—but the great bar of iron was twisted and had taken the form of a bow!

Then Balla Fasséké sang out the "Hymn to the Bow," striking up with his powerful voice:

"Take your bow, Simbon,
Take your bow and let us go.
Take your bow, Sogolon Djata."

When Sogolon saw her son standing she stood dumb for a moment, then suddenly she sang these words of thanks to God, who had given her son the use of his legs:

"Oh day, what a beautiful day,
Oh day, day of joy;
Allah[9] Almighty, you never created a finer day.
So my son is going to walk!"

Standing in the position of a soldier at ease, Sogolon Djata, supported by his enormous rod, was sweating great beads of sweat. Balla Fasséké's song had alerted the whole palace and people came running from all over to see what had happened, and each stood bewildered before Sogolon's son. The queen mother had rushed there and when she saw Mari Djata standing up she trembled from head to foot. After recovering his breath Sogolon's son dropped the bar and the crowd stood to one side. His first steps were those of a giant. Balla Fasséké fell into step and pointing his finger at Djata, he cried:

"Room, room, make room!
The lion has walked;
Hide antelopes,

Get out of his way."
Behind Niani there was a young baobab tree and it was there that the children of the town came to pick leaves for their mothers. With all his might the son of Sogolon tore up the tree and put it on his shoulders and went back to his mother. He threw the tree in front of the hut and said, "Mother, here are some baobab leaves for you. From henceforth it will be outside your hut that the women of Niani will come to stock up."

---

9. Allah (al′ ə) Muslim name for God.

TAKE NOTES

Arthur Becomes King of Britain
from The Once and Future King

by T. H. White

King Pellinore arrived for the important weekend in a high state of flurry.

"I say," he exclaimed, "do you know? Have you heard? Is it a secret, what?"

"Is what a secret, what?" they asked him.

"Why, the King," cried his majesty. "You know, about the King?"

"What's the matter with the King?" inquired Sir Ector. "You don't say he's comin' down to hunt with those darned hounds of his or anythin' like that?"

"He's dead," cried King Pellinore tragically. "He's dead, poor fellah, and can't hunt any more."

Sir Grummore stood up respectfully and took off his cap of maintenance.

"The King is dead," he said. "Long live the King."

Everybody else felt they ought to stand up too, and the boys' nurse burst into tears.

"There, there," she sobbed. "His loyal highness dead and gone, and him such a respectful gentleman. Many's the illuminated picture I've cut out of him, from the Illustrated Missals,[1] aye, and stuck up over the mantel. From the time when he was in swaddling bands,[2] right through them world towers till he was a-visiting the dispersed areas as the world's Prince Charming, there wasn't a picture of 'im but I had it out, aye, and give 'im a last thought o' nights."

"Compose yourself, Nannie," said Sir Ector.

"It is solemn, isn't it?" said King Pellinore, "what? Uther the Conqueror, 1066 to 1216."

"A solemn moment," said Sir Grummore. "The King is dead. Long live the King."

---

1. **Missals** (mis´ əlz) *n.* books produced by the Roman Catholic Church for solemn religious purposes.
2. **swaddling** (swäd´ 'l iŋ) **bands** in former times, long, narrow bands of cloth wrapped around a newborn baby.

"We ought to pull down the curtains," said Kay, who was always a stickler for good form, "or half-mast[3] the banners."

"That's right," said Sir Ector. "Somebody go and tell the sergeant-at-arms."

It was obviously the Wart's[4] duty to execute this command, for he was now the junior nobleman present, so he ran out cheerfully to find the sergeant. Soon those who were left in the solar[5] could hear a voice crying out, "Nah then, one-two, special mourning fer 'is lite majesty, lower awai on the command Two!" and then the flapping of all the standards, banners, pennons, pennoncells, banderolls, guidons, streamers and cognizances[6] which made gay the snowy turrets of the Forest Sauvage.

"How did you hear?" asked Sir Ector.

"I was pricking through the purlieus[7] of the forest after that Beast, you know, when I met with a solemn friar of orders gray, and he told me. It's the very latest news."

"Poor old Pendragon," said Sir Ector.

"The King is dead," said Sir Grummore solemnly. "Long live the King."

"It is all very well for you to keep on mentioning that, my dear Grummore," exclaimed King Pellinore petulantly, "but who is this King, what, that is to live so long, what, accordin' to you?"

"Well, his heir," said Sir Grummore, rather taken aback.

"Our blessed monarch," said the Nurse tearfully, "never had no hair. Anybody that studied the loyal family knowed that."

"Good gracious!" exclaimed Sir Ector. "But he must have had a next-of-kin?"

"That's just it," cried King Pellinore in high excitement. "That's the excitin' part of it, what? No hair and no next of skin, and who's to succeed to the throne? That's what my friar was so excited about,

---

3. **half-mast** *v.* lower a flag halfway down a pole as a sign of mourning.
4. **the Wart's** In this novel, Arthur's childhood nickname is the Wart.
5. **solar** (sō´ lər) *n.* sun room.
6. **standards . . . cognizances** (käg´ nə zən´ səz) banners or flags.
7. **purlieus** (purl´ yōōz´) *n.* outlying part of a forest, in which forest laws were not enforced.

TAKE NOTES

TAKE NOTES

what, and why he was asking who could succeed to what, what? What?"

"Do you mean to tell me," exclaimed Sir Grummore indignantly, "that there ain't no King of Gramarye?"

"Not a scrap of one," cried King Pellinore, feeling important. "And there have been signs and wonders of no mean might."

"I think it's a scandal," said Sir Grummore. "God knows what the dear old country is comin' to. Due to these lollards and communists, no doubt."

"What sort of signs and wonders?" asked Sir Ector.

"Well, there has appeared a sort of sword in a stone, what, in a sort of a church. Not in the church, if you see what I mean, and not in the stone, but that sort of thing, what, like you might say."

"I don't know what the Church is coming to," said Sir Grummore.

"It's in an anvil,"[8] explained the King.

"The Church?"

"No, the sword."

"But I thought you said the sword was in the stone?"

"No," said King Pellinore. "The stone is outside the church."

"Look here, Pellinore," said Sir Ector. "You have a bit of a rest, old boy, and start again. Here, drink up this horn of mead[9] and take it easy."

"The sword," said King Pellinore, "is stuck through an anvil which stands on a stone. It goes right through the anvil and into the stone. The anvil is stuck to the stone. The stone stands outside a church. Give me some more mead."

"I don't think that's much of a wonder," remarked Sir Grummore. "What I wonder at is that they should allow such things to happen. But you can't tell nowadays, what with all these Saxon agitators."[10]

"My dear fellah," cried Pellinore, getting excited again, "it's not where the stone is, what, that I'm trying to tell you, but what is written on it, what, where it is."

"What?"

---

8. **anvil** (anʹ vəl) *n.* iron or steel block on which a blacksmith rests metal to hammer it into shape.

9. **mead** (mēd) *n.* drink made of fermented honey and water.

10. **Saxon** (sakʹ sən) **agitators** (ajʹ i tātʹ ərz) The Saxons were a Germanic people who conquered parts of England during the early centuries of the Middle Ages. Agitators are people who stir up trouble.

"Why, on its pommel."[11]

"Come on, Pellinore," said Sir Ector. "You just sit quite still with your face to the wall for a minute, and then tell us what you are talkin' about. Take it easy, old boy. No need for hurryin'. You sit still and look at the wall, there's a good chap, and talk as slow as you can."

"There are words written on this sword in this stone outside this church," cried King Pellinore piteously, "and these words are as follows. Oh, do try to listen to me, you two, instead of interruptin' all the time about nothin', for it makes a man's head go ever so."

"What are these words?" asked Kay.

"These words say this," said King Pellinore, "so far as I can understand from that old friar of orders gray."

"Go on, do," said Kay, for the King had come to a halt.

"Go on," said Sir Ector, "what do these words on this sword in this anvil in this stone outside this church, say?"

"Some red propaganda, no doubt," remarked Sir Grummore.

King Pellinore closed his eyes tight, extended his arms in both directions, and announced in capital letters, "Whoso Pulleth Out This Sword of this Stone and Anvil, is Rightwise King Born of All England."

"Who said that?" asked Sir Grummore.

"But the sword said it, like I tell you."

"Talkative weapon," remarked Sir Grummore skeptically.

"It was written on it," cried the King angrily. "Written on it in letters of gold."

"Why didn't you pull it out then?" asked Sir Grummore.

"But I tell you that I wasn't there. All this that I am telling you was told to me by that friar I was telling you of, like I tell you."

"Has this sword with this inscription been pulled out?" inquired Sir Ector.

"No," whispered King Pellinore dramatically. "That's where the whole excitement comes in. They can't pull this sword out at all, although they have all been

---

11. pommel (päm´ əl) *n.* knob at the end of the hilt of some swords.

TAKE NOTES

tryin' like fun, and so they have had to proclaim a tournament all over England, for New Year's Day, so that the man who comes to the tournament and pulls out the sword can be King of all England forever, what, I say?"

"Oh, father," cried Kay. "The man who pulls the sword out of the stone will be the King of England. Can't we go to the tournament, father, and have a shot?"

"Couldn't think of it," said Sir Ector.

"Long way to London," said Sir Grummore, shaking his head.

"My father went there once," said King Pellinore.

Kay said, "Oh, surely we could go? When I am knighted I shall have to go to a tournament somewhere, and this one happens at just the right date. All the best people will be there, and we should see the famous knights and great kings. It does not matter about the sword, of course, but think of the tournament, probably the greatest there has ever been in Gramarye, and all the things we should see and do. Dear father, let me go to this tourney, if you love me, so that I may bear away the prize of all, in my maiden fight."

"But, Kay," said Sir Ector, "I have never been to London."

"All the more reason to go. I believe that anybody who does not go for a tournament like this will be proving that he has no noble blood in his veins. Think what people will say about us, if we do not go and have a shot at that sword. They will say that Sir Ector's family was too vulgar and knew it had no chance."

"We all know the family has no chance," said Sir Ector, "that is, for the sword."

"Lot of people in London," remarked Sir Grummore, with a wild surmise. "So they say."

He took a deep breath and goggled at his host with eyes like marbles.

"And shops," added King Pellinore suddenly, also beginning to breathe heavily.

"Dang it!" cried Sir Ector, bumping his horn mug on the table so that it spilled. "Let's all go to London, then, and see the new King!"

They rose up as one man.

"Why shouldn't I be as good a man as my father?" exclaimed King Pellinore.

"Dash it all," cried Sir Grummore. "After all, it is the capital!"

"Hurray!" shouted Kay.

"Lord have mercy," said the nurse.

At this moment the Wart came in with Merlyn, and everybody was too excited to notice that, if he had not been grown up now, he would have been on the verge of tears.

"Oh, Wart," cried Kay, forgetting for the moment that he was only addressing his squire, and slipping back into the familiarity of their boyhood. "What do you think? We are all going to London for a great tournament on New Year's Day!"

"Are we?"

"Yes, and you will carry my shield and spears for the jousts, and I shall win the palm[12] of everybody and be a great knight!"

"Well, I am glad we are going," said the Wart, "for Merlyn is leaving us too."

"Oh, we shan't need Merlyn."

"He is leaving us," repeated the Wart.

"Leavin' us?" asked Sir Ector. "I thought it was we that were leavin'?"

"He is going away from the Forest Sauvage."

Sir Ector said, "Come now, Merlyn, what's all this about? I don't understand all this a bit."

"I have come to say Goodbye, Sir Ector," said the old magician. "Tomorrow my pupil Kay will be knighted, and the next week my other pupil will go away as his squire. I have outlived my usefulness here, and it is time to go."

"Now, now, don't say that," said Sir Ector. "I think you're a jolly useful chap whatever happens. You just stay and teach me, or be the librarian or something. Don't you leave an old man alone, after the children have flown."

"We shall all meet again," said Merlyn. "There is no cause to be sad."

"Don't go," said Kay.

"I must go," replied their tutor. "We have had a good time while we were young, but it is in the nature of

---

12. win the palm be the winner. A palm leaf is a symbol of victory.

TAKE NOTES

Time to fly. There are many things in other parts of the kingdom which I ought to be attending to just now, and it is a specially busy time for me. Come, Archimedes,[13] say Goodbye to the company."

"Goodbye," said Archimedes tenderly to the Wart.

"Goodbye," said the Wart without looking up at all.

"But you can't go," cried Sir Ector, "not without a month's notice."

"Can't I?" replied Merlyn, taking up the position always used by philosophers who propose to dematerialize. He stood on his toes, while Archimedes held tight to his shoulder—began to spin on them slowly like a top—spun faster and faster till he was only a blur of grayish light—and in a few seconds there was no one there at all.

"Goodbye, Wart," cried two faint voices outside the solar window.

"Goodbye," said the Wart for the last time—and the poor fellow went quickly out of the room.

The knighting took place in a whirl of preparations. Kay's sumptuous bath had to be set up in the box room, between two towel-horses and an old box of selected games which contained a wornout straw dartboard—it was called fléchette in those days—because all the other rooms were full of packing. The nurse spent the whole time constructing new warm pants for everybody, on the principle that the climate of any place outside the Forest Sauvage must be treacherous to the extreme, and, as for the sergeant, he polished all the armor till it was quite brittle and sharpened the swords till they were almost worn away.

At last it was time to set out.

Perhaps, if you happen not to have lived in the Old England of the twelfth century, or whenever it was, and in a remote castle on the borders of the Marches at that, you will find it difficult to imagine the wonders of their journey.

The road, or track, ran most of the time along the high ridges of the hills or downs, and they could look down on either side of them upon the desolate marshes where the snowy reeds sighed, and the ice crackled, and the duck in the red sunsets quacked loud on the

---

13. **Archimedes** (är´ kə mē´ dēz´) Merlin's owl, who is able to talk.

winter air. The whole country was like that. Perhaps there would be a moory marsh on one side of the ridge, and a forest of a hundred thousand acres on the other, with all the great branches weighted in white. They could sometimes see a wisp of smoke among the trees, or a huddle of buildings far out among the impassable reeds, and twice they came to quite respectable towns which had several inns to boast of, but on the whole it was an England without civilization. The better roads were cleared of cover for a bow-shot on either side of them, lest the traveler should be slain by hidden thieves.

They slept where they could, sometimes in the hut of some cottager who was prepared to welcome them, sometimes in the castle of a brother knight who invited them to refresh themselves, sometimes in the firelight and fleas of a dirty little hovel with a bush tied to a pole outside it—this was the signboard used at that time by inns—and once or twice on the open ground, all huddled together for warmth between their grazing chargers. Wherever they went and wherever they slept, the east wind whistled in the reeds, and the geese went over high in the starlight, honking at the stars.

London was full to the brim. If Sir Ector had not been lucky enough to own a little land in Pie Street, on which there stood a respectable inn, they would have been hard put to it to find a lodging. But he did own it, and as a matter of fact drew most of his dividends from that source, so they were able to get three beds between the five of them. They thought themselves fortunate.

On the first day of the tournament, Sir Kay managed to get them on the way to the lists at least an hour before the jousts could possibly begin. He had lain awake all night, imagining how he was going to beat the best barons in England, and he had not been able to eat his breakfast. Now he rode at the front of the cavalcade, with pale cheeks, and Wart wished there was something he could do to calm him down.

For country people, who only knew the dismantled tilting ground[14] of Sir Ector's castle, the scene which

---

14. tilting ground ground on which a joust takes place.

TAKE NOTES

met their eyes was ravishing. It was a huge green pit in the earth, about as big as the arena at a football match. It lay ten feet lower than the surrounding country, with sloping banks, and the snow had been swept off it. It had been kept warm with straw, which had been cleared off that morning, and now the close-worn grass sparkled green in the white landscape. Round the arena there was a world of color so dazzling and moving and twinkling as to make one blink one's eyes. The wooden grandstands were painted in scarlet and white. The silk pavilions of famous people, pitched on every side, were azure and green and saffron and checkered. The pennons and pennoncells which floated everywhere in the sharp wind were flapping with every color of the rainbow, as they strained and slapped at their flagpoles, and the barrier down the middle of the arena itself was done in chessboard squares of black and white. Most of the combatants and their friends had not yet arrived, but one could see from those few who had come how the very people would turn the scene into a bank of flowers, and how the armor would flash, and the scalloped sleeves of the heralds jig in the wind, as they raised their brazen trumpets to their lips to shake the fleecy clouds of winter with joyances[15] and fanfares.

"Good heavens!" cried Sir Kay. "I have left my sword at home."

"Can't joust without a sword," said Sir Grummore. "Quite irregular."

"Better go and fetch it," said Sir Ector. "You have time."

"My squire will do," said Sir Kay. "What an awful mistake to make! Here, squire, ride hard back to the inn and fetch my sword. You shall have a shilling[16] if you fetch it in time."

The Wart went as pale as Sir Kay was, and looked as if he were going to strike him. Then he said, "It shall be done, master," and turned his ambling palfrey[17] against the stream of newcomers. He began to push his way toward their hostelry[18] as best he might.

---

15. **joyances** (joi′ əns iz) *n.* old word meaning "rejoicing."
16. **shilling** (shil′ iŋ) *n.* British silver coin.
17. **palfrey** (pôl′ frē) *n.* old term for a saddle horse, especially one for women.
18. **hostelry** (häs′ təl rē) *n.* inn.

"To offer me money!" cried the Wart to himself. "To look down at this beastly little donkey-affair off his great charger and to call me Squire! Oh, Merlyn, give me patience with the brute, and stop me from throwing his filthy shilling in his face."

When he got to the inn it was closed. Everybody had thronged to see the famous tournament, and the entire household had followed after the mob. Those were lawless days and it was not safe to leave your house— or even to go to sleep in it—unless you were certain that it was impregnable.[19] The wooden shutters bolted over the downstairs windows were two inches thick, and the doors were double-barred.

"Now what do I do," asked the Wart, "to earn my shilling?"

He looked ruefully at the blind little inn, and began to laugh.

"Poor Kay," he said. "All that shilling stuff was only because he was scared and miserable, and now he has good cause to be. Well, he shall have a sword of some sort if I have to break into the Tower of London.

"How does one get hold of a sword?" he continued. "Where can I steal one? Could I waylay some knight, even if I am mounted on an ambling pad, and take his weapons by force? There must be some swordsmith or armorer in a great town like this, whose shop would be still open."

He turned his mount and cantered off along the street. There was a quiet churchyard at the end of it, with a kind of square in front of the church door. In the middle of the square there was a heavy stone with an anvil on it, and a fine new sword was stuck through the anvil.

"Well," said the Wart, "I suppose it is some sort of war memorial, but it will have to do. I am sure nobody would grudge Kay a war memorial, if they knew his desperate straits."

He tied his reins round a post of the lych gate,[20] strode up the gravel path, and took hold of the sword.

"Come, sword," he said. "I must cry your mercy and take you for a better cause.

---

19. **impregnable** (im preg' nə bəl) *adj.* not capable of being captured or entered by force.
20. **lych** (lich) **gate** roofed gate at the entrance to a churchyard.

TAKE NOTES

TAKE NOTES

"This is extraordinary," said the Wart. "I feel strange when I have hold of this sword, and I notice everything much more clearly. Look at the beautiful gargoyles[21] of the church, and of the monastery which it belongs to. See how splendidly all the famous banners in the aisle are waving. How nobly that yew[22] holds up the red flakes of its timbers to worship God. How clean the snow is. I can smell something like fetherfew and sweet briar—and is it music that I hear?"

It was music, whether of pan-pipes or of recorders, and the light in the churchyard was so clear, without being dazzling, that one could have picked a pin out twenty yards away.

"There is something in this place," said the Wart. "There are people. Oh, people, what do you want?"

Nobody answered him, but the music was loud and the light beautiful.

"People," cried the Wart, "I must take this sword. It is not for me, but for Kay. I will bring it back."

There was still no answer, and Wart turned back to the anvil. He saw the golden letters, which he did not read, and the jewels on the pommel, flashing in the lovely light.

"Come, sword," said the Wart.

He took hold of the handles with both hands, and strained against the stone. There was a melodious consort[23] on the recorders, but nothing moved.

The Wart let go of the handles, when they were beginning to bite into the palms of his hands, and stepped back, seeing stars.

"It is well fixed," he said.

He took hold of it again and pulled with all his might. The music played more strongly, and the light all about the churchyard glowed like amethysts; but the sword still stuck.

"Oh, Merlyn," cried the Wart, "help me to get this weapon."

There was a kind of rushing noise, and a long chord played along with it. All round the churchyard there were hundreds of old friends. They rose over the church

---

21. **gargoyles** (gär´ goilz´) *n.* grotesque sculptures of animals or fantastic creatures decorating a building.
22. **yew** (yo͞o) *n.* type of evergreen tree with red cones.
23. **consort** (kän´ sôrt´) *n.* piece of music composed for a small group.

wall all together, like the Punch-and-Judy[24] ghosts of remembered days, and there were badgers and nightingales and vulgar crows and hares and wild geese and falcons and fishes and dogs and dainty unicorns and solitary wasps and corkindrills and hedgehogs and griffins and the thousand other animals he had met. They loomed round the church wall, the lovers and helpers of the Wart, and they all spoke solemnly in turn. Some of them had come from the banners in the church, where they were painted in heraldry, some from the waters and the sky and the fields about— but all, down to the smallest shrew mouse, had come to help on account of love. Wart felt his power grow.

"Put your back into it," said a luce (or pike) off one of the heraldic banners, "as you once did when I was going to snap you up. Remember that power springs from the nape of the neck."

"What about those forearms," asked a badger gravely, "that are held together by a chest? Come along, my dear embryo,[25] and find your tool."

A merlin sitting at the top of the yew tree cried out, "Now then, Captain Wart, what is the first law of the foot? I thought I once heard something about never letting go."

"Don't work like a stalling woodpecker," urged a tawny owl affectionately. "Keep up a steady effort, my duck, and you will have it yet."

A white-front said. "Now, Wart, if you were once able to fly the great North Sea, surely you can coordinate a few little wing-muscles here and there? Fold your powers together, with the spirit of your mind, and it will come out like butter. Come along, Homo sapiens,[26] for all we humble friends of yours are waiting here to cheer."

The Wart walked up to the great sword for the third time. He put out his right hand softly and drew it out as gently as from a scabbard.

There was a lot of cheering, a noise like a hurdy-gurdy[27] which went on and on. In the middle of this

---

24. **Punch-and-Judy** puppets of the quarrelsome Punch and his wife, Judy, who fight constantly in a comical way.
25. **embryo** (em′ brē ō′) *n.* anything in an early stage of development.
26. **Homo sapiens** (hō′ mō sā′ pē enz′) scientific name for human beings.
27. **hurdy-gurdy** (hʉr′ dē gʉr′ dē) *n.* musical instrument played by turning a crank.

Arthur Becomes King of Britain *from* The Once and Future King **185**

TAKE NOTES

noise, after a long time, he saw Kay and gave him the sword. The people at the tournament were making a frightful row.

"But this is not my sword," said Sir Kay.

"It was the only one I could get," said the Wart. "The inn was locked."

"It is a nice-looking sword. Where did you get it?"

"I found it stuck in a stone, outside a church."

Sir Kay had been watching the tilting nervously, waiting for his turn. He had not paid much attention to his squire.

"That is a funny place to find one," he said.

"Yes, it was stuck through an anvil."

"What?" cried Sir Kay, suddenly rounding upon him. "Did you just say this sword was stuck in a stone?"

"It was," said the Wart. "It was a sort of war memorial."

Sir Kay stared at him for several seconds in amazement, opened his mouth, shut it again, licked his lips, then turned his back and plunged through the crowd. He was looking for Sir Ector, and the Wart followed after him.

"Father," cried Sir Kay, "come here a moment."

"Yes, my boy," said Sir Ector. "Splendid falls these professional chaps do manage. Why, what's the matter, Kay? You look as white as a sheet."

"Do you remember that sword which the King of England would pull out?"

"Yes."

"Well, here it is. I have it. It is in my hand. I pulled it out."

Sir Ector did not say anything silly. He looked at Kay and he looked at the Wart. Then he stared at Kay again, long and lovingly, and said, "We will go back to the church."

"Now then, Kay," he said, when they were at the church door. He looked at his firstborn kindly, but straight between the eyes. "Here is the stone, and you have the sword. It will make you the King of England. You are my son that I am proud of, and always will be, whatever you do. Will you promise me that you took it out by your own might?"

Kay looked at his father. He also looked at the Wart and at the sword.

Then he handed the sword to the Wart quite quietly. He said, "I am a liar. Wart pulled it out."

As far as the Wart was concerned, there was a time after this in which Sir Ector kept telling him to put the sword back into the stone—which he did—and in which Sir Ector and Kay then vainly tried to take it out. The Wart took it out for them, and stuck it back again once or twice. After this, there was another time which was more painful.

He saw that his dear guardian was looking quite old and powerless, and that he was kneeling down with difficulty on a gouty[28] knee.

"Sir," said Sir Ector, without looking up, although he was speaking to his own boy.

"Please do not do this, father," said the Wart, kneeling down also. "Let me help you up, Sir Ector, because you are making me unhappy."

"Nay, nay, my lord," said Sir Ector, with some very feeble old tears. "I was never your father nor of your blood, but I wote[29] well ye are of an higher blood than I wend[30] ye were."

"Plenty of people have told me you are not my father," said the Wart, "but it does not matter a bit."

"Sir," said Sir Ector humbly, "will ye be my good and gracious lord when ye are King?"

"Don't!" said the Wart.

"Sir," said Sir Ector, "I will ask no more of you but that you will make my son, your foster-brother, Sir Kay, seneschal[31] of all your lands?"

Kay was kneeling down too, and it was more than the Wart could bear.

"Oh, do stop," he cried. "Of course he can be seneschal, if I have got to be this King, and, oh, father, don't kneel down like that, because it breaks my heart. Please get up, Sir Ector, and don't make everything so horrible. Oh, dear, oh, dear, I wish I had never seen that filthy sword at all."

And the Wart also burst into tears.

---

28. **gouty** (gout′ ē) *adj.* having gout, a disease causing swelling and severe pain in the joints.
29. **wote** (wōt) *v.* old word meaning "know."
30. **wend** (wend) *v.* thought (past tense of *ween,* an old word meaning "think").
31. **seneschal** (sen′ ə shəl) *n.* steward, or manager, in the house of a medieval noble.

Grateful acknowledgment is made to the following for copyrighted material:

Cornelius Eady "The Empty Dance Shoes" and "The Poetic Interpretation of the Twist" by Cornelius Eady from *Victims of the Latest Dance Craze: Poems by Cornelius Eady.* Copyright © 1985 by Cornelius Eady. All rights reserved. Used by permission.

Farrar, Straus & Giroux "The Fish" by Elizabeth Bishop from *The Complete Poems 1927-1979.* Copyright © 1979, 1983 by Alice Helen Methfessel.

Harcourt, Inc. "How to React to Familiar Faces" from *How to Travel with a Salmon & Other Essays* by Umberto Eco, copyright © Gruppo Editoriale Fabbri, Bompiani, Sonzogno, Etas S.p.A., English translation by William Weaver copyright © 1994 by Harcourt, Inc. "Jazz Fantasia" by Carl Sandburg from *Smoke and Steel.* Copyright © 1920 by Harcourt, Inc. and renewed 1948 by Carl Sandburg. "Antigone" by Sophocles from *Sophocles: The Oedipus Cycle, An English Version.* The Oedipus Cycle: An English Version by Dudley Fitts and Robert Fitzgerald, copyright © 1939 by Harcourt Inc., and renewed 1967 by Dudley Fitts and Robert Fitzgerald. This material may not be reproduced in any form or by any means without the prior written permission of the publisher. **CAUTION:** All rights, including professional, amateur, motion picture, recitation, lecturing, performance, public reading, radio broadcasting, and television are strictly reserved. Inquiries of all rights should be addressed to Harcourt, Inc., Permissions Dept., Orlando, FL 32887. Used by permission of the publisher.

Harper's Magazine "The Leap" by Louise Erdrich from *Harper's Magazine.* Copyright © 1990 by Harper's Magazine Foundation. Used from the March issue by special permission.

Harvard University Press "The Wind-tapped like a tired man (#436)" by Emily Dickinson from *The Poems of Emily Dickinson*, Thomas H. Johnson, ed., Cambridge, Mass.: The Belknap Press of Harvard University Press, Copyright © 1951, 1955, 1979, 1983 by the President and Fellows of Harvard College. Used by permission of the publishers and the Trustees of Amherst College. Copyright © 1951, 1955, by the President and Fellows of Harvard College. © Copyright 1914, 1918, 1919, 1924, 1929, 1930, 1932, 1935, 1937, 1942 by Martha Dickinson Bianchi.

Hispanic Society of America "The Guitar" by Federico García Lorca from *Translations From Hispanic Poets.* Copyright 1938 by The Hispanic Society of America. Used with permission of the Hispanic Society of America.

Houghton Mifflin Company, Inc. "Prometheus and the First People" (originally titled "The Creation of Man" and "The Coming of Evil") from *Greek Myths* by Olivia E. Coolidge. Copyright © 1949 by Olivia E. Coolidge; copyright renewed © 1977 by Olivia E. Coolidge. Adapted by permission of Houghton Mifflin Company. Text © 1949 by Olivia E. Coolidge. Used by permission of Houghton Mifflin Co. All rights reserved.

Johnson & Alcock Ltd., London "The Bridegroom" by Alexander Pushkin from *The Bronze Horseman and Other Poems*, Secker & Warburg, 1982. Translation © D.M. Thomas. Used by permission of Johnson and Alcock Ltd., London.

Alfred A. Knopf, Inc. "The Weary Blues" by Langston Hughes from *Selected Poems of Langston Hughes*, copyright © 1994 by The Estate of Langston Hughes. Copyright © 1926 Alfred A. Knopf, Inc., Renewed 1954 Estate of Langston Hughes. Used by permission of Alfred A. Knopf, a division of Random House, Inc. All rights reserved.

Liveright Publishing Corporation "Reapers" by Jean Toomer from *Cane.* Copyright 1923 by Boni & Liveright, renewed 1951 by Jean Toomer. Used by permission of Liveright Publishing Corporation.

New American Library, a division of Penguin "An Enemy of the People" by Henrik Ibsen from *The Complete Major Prose Plays of Henrik Ibsen* translated by Rolf Fjelde, copyright © 1965, 1970, 1978 by Rolf Fjelde. Used by permission of Dutton Signet, a division of Penguin Group (USA) Inc.

New Directions Publishing Corporation "Do Not Go Gentle into That Good Night" by Dylan Thomas from *The Poems of Dylan Thomas.* Copyright © 1952 by Dylan Thomas. "A Tree Telling of Orpheus" by Denise Levertov from *Poems, 1968-1972.* Copyright © 1965, 1966, 1967,1968, 1969, 1970, 1971 by Denise Levertov Goodman. Copyright © 1970, 1971, 1972, 1987 by Denise Levertov. Used by permission of New Directions Publishing Corp.

Norwegian Nobel Institute Keep Memory Alive by Elie Wiesel from *Elie Wiesel's Nobel Prize Acceptance Speech.* Used with permission from the Norwegian Nobel Institute. Copyright © 1986 by the Nobel Foundation.

Naomi Shihab Nye "Making a Fist" by Naomi Shihab Nye from *Hugging the Jukebox.* Copyright © 1982 by Dutton: New York. Used by permission of the author, Naomi Shihab Nye.

Pearson Education Ltd. From "Sundiata: An Epic of Old Mali: Childhood, The Lion's Awakening" by D.T. Niane translated by G.D. Pickett from *Sundiata: An Epic of Old Mali.* Copyright © Longman Group Limited 1965, used by permission of Pearson Education Limited. Copyright © Presence Africaine 1960 (original French version: Soundjata, ou L'Epopee Mandingue) © Longman Group Ltd. (English Version) 1965.

Penguin Group (USA) Inc. "Everest" from *Touch the Top of the World: A Blind Man's Journey to Climb Farther than the Eye Can See* by Erik Weihenmayer. Copyright © 2002 by Erik Weihenmayer. All rights reserved.

G.P. Putnam's Sons, a division of Penguin "Arthur Becomes King" Part I, Chapter XXII from *The Once and Future King* by T.H. White. Copyright © 1938, 1939, 1940, © 1958 by T. H. White, renewed.

Marian Reiner, Literary Agent "Metaphor" by Eve Merriam from *It Doesn't Always Have to Rhyme*. Copyright © 1964, 1970, 1973, 1986 by Eve Merriam. Used by permission of Marian Reiner.

Rogers, Coleridge and White, Ltd. "Games at Twilight" by Anita Desai from *Games at Twilight and Other Stories*. Copyright © 1978 by Anita Desai. Used by permission of the author c/o Rogers, Coleridge & White Ltd., 20 Powis Mews, London W11 1JN.

Heyden White Rostow "The American Idea" by Theodore H. White from *The New York Times Magazine, July 6, 1986*. Copyright © 1986 by Theodore H. White. Copyright © 1986 by The New York Times Company. All rights reserved. Used by permission.

The Sheep Meadow Press "Pride" by Dahlia Ravikovitch translated by Chana Bloch and Ariel Bloch from *The Window*. Copyright © 1987 by Chana Bloch. All rights reserved. Used by permission.

Anthony Thwaite "Tanka: "Was it that I went to sleep"" by Ono no Komachi translated and co-edited by Geoffrey Bownas and Anthony Thwaite from *The Penguin Book of Japanese Verse*. "One cannot ask loneliness" by Priest Jakuren translated by Bownas & Thwaite from *The Penguin Book of Japanese Verse*. Penguin Books copyright © 1964, revised edition 1998. Translation copyright © Geoffrey Bownas and Anthony Thwaite, 1964, 1998. Used by permission.

University of North Carolina Press The Street of the Canon" by Josefina Niggli from *Mexican Village*. Copyright © 1945 by the University of North Carolina Press, renewed 1972 by Josefina Niggli. Used by permission of the publisher.

Viking Penguin, Inc. "My City" by James Weldon Johnson from *Saint Peter Relates an Incident*. Copyright © 1935 by James Weldon "Johnson," © renewed 1963 by Grace Nail Johnson. All rights reserved.

Wesleyan University Press "Glory" by Yusef Komunyakaa from *Magic City* (Wesleyan University Press, 1992) Copyright © 1992 by Yusef Komunyakaa and used by permission of Wesleyan University Press.